ENDS OF THE EARTH

ENDS OF THE EARTH
Some Collected Travels

BY

PETER DUVAL SMITH

WITH AN INTRODUCTION BY
JAMES CAMERON

HAMISH HAMILTON

LONDON

*First Published in Great Britain
by Hamish Hamilton Ltd 1969
90 Great Russell Street London W.C.1*

SBN 241 01736 X

COPYRIGHT NOTICE

© 1969 by Pamela Duval Smith

All rights reserved. No part of this publication may be reproduced, stored in a retrieval system, or transmitted, in any form or by any means, electronic, mechanical, photocopying, recording or otherwise, without prior permission of the Copyright owner.

*Printed in Great Britain by
Western Printing Services Ltd Bristol*

'I arrived in Avignon with that small excited feeling in the pit of my stomach that is one of the nicest feelings there is.'

Peter Duval Smith

CONTENTS

Introduction   xi

PART ONE
SOUTH AMERICA

1. The City in the Jungle   1
2. The Worst Place in the World   7
3. The Smugglers' Express   14
4. The New People   21
5. On the River Sea   26
6. The Day of the Radishes   32

PART TWO
EUROPE

7. Finland: The Russian Excursion   38
8. Sweden: The Perils of Affluence   44
9. Germany: Berlin by Night   50
10. Poland: The Cool Generation   56
11. Germany: Taking the Waters, Playing the Tables   62
12. Switzerland: Where the Money Is   68
13. Greece: The Real Greece   74
14. Italy: Venice Revealed   80
15. France: In Search of Wild Horses   86
16. Spain: What Next?   92
17. Thoughts After Europe   98

PART THREE
AFRICA

18. Ethiopia: Journey to Harar   104
19. Ethiopia: A Schoolboy's Tour of Addis   109

20. Ethiopia: Morning in the Piazza	115
21. Ethiopia: At Mama's Place	121
22. South West Africa: Skeleton Coast	126
23. Egypt: The Black Museum	132
24. Ghana: I Fell into a Storm Drain	138

PART FOUR
HERE AND THERE

25. Five Stars Around the World	144
26. Letter from Iceland	148
27. Hearts and Minds	154
28. To Fly from Christmas	161
29. Conrad on the Spot	167
30. The Pleasure of Contrast	171

EDITOR'S NOTE

WE would like to thank Mrs. Pamela Duval Smith for permission to publish these talks, all of which were originally broadcast by the BBC during the last eight years on what used to be the Home Service and is now Radio 4.

We would also like to acknowledge the Corporation's part in commissioning these talks in the first place. As James Cameron points out in his introduction, Peter's forte—the two-thousand-word essay—is a form now almost unique to sound radio so that it is literally true to say that without the BBC most of these pieces would never have appeared.

Peter spent the greater part of his professional life with the BBC, first as a Producer and afterwards as a contributor to their output in almost every field, so that these particular talks reflect only a small part of his broadcast work over the years. However I think they represent the best part and certainly they are the most typical expression of his relaxed, inquisitive outlook.

The lines from Roy Campbell's poem 'Horses on the Camargue' and the excerpt from Conrad's story 'The Secret Sharer' are used here with the permission respectively of Curtis Brown Ltd. on behalf of the Roy Campbell Estate, and the Trustees of the Joseph Conrad Estate and J. M. Dent and Sons Ltd.

JOSEPH HONE

INTRODUCTION BY
JAMES CAMERON

To read these widely different, serious, funny, touching, mordant pieces of writing in collection for the first time brings a curious urge to say: they don't come like that any more; this is the kind of work we rarely see these days from the new men. And then one realizes—or I realize, which is more to the point—that Peter Duval Smith was indeed himself one of the new men, his work specifically born of the microphone age; he more than most especially belonged to this time. It is my generation they don't make any more of. Peter's endures, though he himself untimely lost.

It is not easy to find a name that precisely defines these pieces. They are of course radio journalism, though the phrase is absurdly inadequate. The broadcast talk, especially in this manner, is probably just about the last form of what was once the Essay—a communication personal and idiosyncratic, informative when information was integral to the style but never instructive, conveying the flavour of the man and that of his subject, in that order. Contemporary printed journalism, it seems to me, has almost abandoned interest in this sort of thing. Reportage tends to be teamwork now, systematized and solid and slightly threatening and touched with the mothball smell of the cuttings library, seeking the unrevealing Revelation and the tedious truth. This technique of the corporate correspondence is happily—so far anyhow—almost a technical impossibility in sound radio, where *someone* at least must read the words; the communication is necessarily person to person, with the imperative dimension of the human and individual voice. It is true that here and there the newspapers maintain small writer-sanctuaries where a whiff of personality is preserved, but it is rare now to find printed room for a man to have his say not for what he tells but how he tells it. There are no longer any Robert Lynds or Ian Mackays. And alas there is no longer a Peter Duval Smith.

Some time ago in a rather self-conscious attempt to make sense of the professional treadmill on which Peter and I both served our time I wrote: 'The function of the journalist tends to be re-defined by everyone who enters the trade, since it has no absolutes nor standards and can vary so much in its fundamentals as to constitute a whole spectrum of trades, from the ex-cathedra pronouncements of a Walter Lippmann or a Raymond Aron to the bleak aridity of a *Times* Law Report.

'However, the job basically consists of observing, describing, and sometimes explaining the happenings of the time, and the operative words there are *the time*. Journalism does not concern itself much with the eternal verities, except occasionally by accident. The only excuse for resurrecting articles from a time past is that they are *part of that time*; the reporter's response to a situation is as much a part of the record as the situation itself. . . .'

This is perhaps a laboured way of arguing the genuine value of books like this, which is not wholly that of the pleasure this one gives. I am certain that journalism—in print or sound, it makes no odds—has this peculiar dimension of time, in that however transient or ephemeral it may be even at its best, it is inseparably part of the period in which it was done, encapsulating a moment, a mood, in which the writer cannot but reflect the state of his world.

This is very true of the broadcasts of Peter Duval Smith—even though, paradoxically, it is the timeless character of his pieces that makes their revival so easy, and so agreeable. To many a reporter Peter's job must have seemed enviable indeed. Not for him the rush and scramble of the first edition deadline, a programme poised at the mercy of the unexpected, the fire-brigade pursuit of a breathless incident of which there would really be little to say except 'I was there.' He went about his way collecting experience in his own time and at his own pace, and distilling it into the fastidiously evocative trifles that were his real achievement. As an old colleague I read them with professional admiration and personal delight, with the wry feeling always that Peter could always profit by what would have been a newsman's despair: tranquillity. One gets the impression that if anything had ever actually *happened* during any of Peter's casual sojourns at the ends of the earth it would have been a most annoying distraction to his purpose, which was absorbing places, not datelining them.

Ends of the Earth ' is an appropriate title for this book, though somehow it suggests an attitude rather more momentous than I think Peter Duval Smith would have chosen. 'Loose Ends of the Earth' might better describe the impression he gives of random discovery, of disciplined leisure, of being in no hurry to move from one lucky exploration to the next. It seems to me that what distinguishes his work from most of his contemporaries is its gently sanguine air, almost unfashionably optimistic: if he does not expect the best he at least does not anticipate the worst; there is pretty surely going to be some decent eccentric to have a drink with somewhere, and however unpromising his new backwater it is bound to provide one more dotty aspect of the human condition. His equable good nature goes a good deal further than mine; he was often improbably charitable—claiming, for example, to discern the 'good society' in Brazil. Even in what he called 'The Worst Place in the World' (his candidate was Cayenne; I know other contenders for the title) he found much to satisfy his connoisseur's taste for the quirkish. Even so, he was no roving Pollyanna; he could be acid where necessary, as he was in Berlin, outraged by the infamous Wall—and not so much by the brutality of the East that built it as by the vulgar avarice of the West that exploits it.

If journalism is part of the time-machine, then all this work is very much part of the Sixties, that historical parenthesis which for some has been fraught with uncertainty and regret, but which for Peter was clearly a period of liberation. He was a compulsive traveller, in the sense peculiar to our time, when moving about the earth is increasingly a button-pushing, agent-calling short cut to tedium, making it ever easier to reach with the greatest despatch places of the maximum inconvenience and discomfort. Peter Duval Smith enjoyed it. He relished his magic carpet; it was his life. I think he felt the need to see the world, every inch of it, while it was still there, or, as it turned out, while he was still there. He did his share, and saw his fill, and he wasted nothing.

Like him, I spend my life on the move. All the crazy places he describes I know myself, even to the most obscure and fanciful of them, and I can testify to the skill and wit of his observation. I can recognize very well the charming lunacies of Addis Ababa, the airless lunar fantasies of La Paz, the arid cynicisms of Zurich. This is travel-writing of a special kind—and integral to the style was that it is, of course, the spoken word. These words were written to be heard and not to be read. All of us who have worked in both forms know the carefully mannered difference there is between the techniques of sight and sound. The style came fluently and elegantly to Peter Duval Smith; he wrote in the cadences of descriptive speech, and this is why in these printed words one can hear him still. Fluency was of course not ease; one knows the strain and trial of producing this essence of the spontaneous.

The last time I chanced on a brief encounter with Peter Duval Smith was in New York City, outside the Algonquin Hotel, where I was engaged on some fretful occasion or other and he, as I recall, was preparing a journey to Viet Nam. It was a day of somewhat confused conviviality. Then we went our ways, and by and by Peter was dead in Saigon, and that was the end of his tireless work.

Not quite the end: it was important that the best of it should endure, and here it is.

PART ONE

SOUTH AMERICA

I

The City in the Jungle
[August 1965]

WHY do I travel? This is the question I've been worrying about lately, and of course not getting very far. Still, it's more important to ask questions than to give answers, in the same way as it's more important to be doing something than to have reasons for doing that thing. Wandering about South America this year, I wondered all right from time to time why I was there, but most of the time I was just absorbed in the place. Still, interesting things can get a bit overpowering, sometimes you like to put your feet up and live at a more normal tempo than the restless life of the traveller allows and that's why I was sad at having to leave Manaus after only three days. It's a place I could spend months in and not be bored. Maybe not everyone would be happy in Manaus. Decadent is the word for this town. It is literally decaying. Manaus was a great place in the early years of this century, when rubber first became an important product. The vast natural forests of the Amazon were the main source of the world's rubber for a number of years, and huge fortunes were made in Manaus. The people who had the money were determined to get some fun out of it. They may have been living half-way up a tropical river a thousand miles from the sea, surrounded by jungles, savage Indians and poisonous snakes, but they set to work to turn Manaus into a sort of combination of Athens and Babylon. Great mansions were built, boulevards with vistas, pleasure gardens and stylish public buildings. Inevitably most of these things were copies of the grand life in other, older places. When the rich rubber merchants of Manaus decided they must have some culture up there on the Amazon, they built an exact copy of the Paris Opera House. The building was put together in every detail in France, then taken apart and shipped out to Brazil, every stone and cornice of it. When it came to having to put something on inside this vast and incongruous place, no trouble or money was spared. Enormous fees were offered to great artistes to persuade them to make the lengthy trek out to Brazil. Pavlova danced in the Opera House at Manaus, and Sarah Bernhardt performed in *Phèdre*. Then one day the bottom fell out of the Amazon rubber market. An Englishman, Sir Henry Wickham, smuggled some rubber tree seeds out of Brazil, took them to Kew Gardens and eventually they were transplanted in Malaya. And that was that. The boulevards and grand houses of Manaus fell into disrepair, and the Opera House was abandoned to bats and lizards. Most of Manaus is still a splendid ruin, but the Opera House has been cleaned up, and stands now dominating the town, a marvellous confection in pink and white with a peacock-coloured mosaic dome. The days of Sarah Bernhardt are over and nothing much goes on there now except amateur dramatic performances by the local fire brigade and that kind of thing.

Manaus sleeps in the sun on the edge of the Amazon and I felt utterly at home there. I wish I was there now. I did exactly what I like to do in a foreign city. I'd get up late and breakfast leisurely and superbly on a variety of tropical fruits, papaya or melon or avocado pear and oranges or peaches or bananas with marvellous fresh-ground Brazilian coffee. I'd stroll out then to look at the town, perhaps drifting towards the market, one of the most remarkable in the world. Part of it is afloat on the Amazon, and you walk along boards from one floating stall to the next. There were strange sights all round. On one stall a man would be selling Brazil nuts. They came enclosed in one big nut rather like a coconut. As I pass the man takes a machete, splits the coconut in half with a single blow, and a shower of little nuts rains out. At the next stall, they are selling monkeys and toads and snakes, not as pets but to be eaten. The stall-holder is leading a small crocodile along on a string. It's jaws are tied up with another bit of string in case it takes a piece out of one of his customers. A gorgeous toucan sits in a cage. I wander on to the meat market, which takes place in a vast hall like a railway terminus. It's a weird sight. Manaus is populated by thousands of vultures called urubus. They hop about on the pavements, they stand like sentinels on all the rooftops, and here in the meat market they are everywhere, scampering and shuffling on the floor, fighting for scraps. I walk out into the town and spread myself out on a café terrace, using at least three chairs for my legs and arms in the Brazilian fashion. I look at everybody and they look at me. The tremendous thing about Brazil is the almost complete absence of the usual barriers to human intercourse. It's an almost classless society. A cat may look at a king in Brazil and the king looks back with equal interest. In no time I have a companion. It may be a pretty girl, or a beggar, or the waiter, or a businessman slipped out for a cup of coffee. The day goes on in this pleasant way. I'll have lunch in a restaurant looking out on the street, then a siesta, then another stroll in the town in the exciting airs of a tropical evening. Then I might go to an open-air cinema or a cabaret or even do some work in my room. If I go out for a nightcap, I'll be certain to find company, in the street or a café or a bar, at whatever time of night. It'll be easy company, boring or amusing, but always friendly and natural.

If one wonders why one travels, here in Manaus is surely one of the answers. Of course there is plenty wrong with Manaus, but not things that really matter. The electricity is always failing and the telephones don't work. The pavements are falling to bits and crossing the road is an adventure. There is rubbish lying everywhere. People push and jostle you. It's very hot and it rains all the time. The whole place smells like an unmade bed. Never mind: even the defects are mostly due to the sort of excess of humanity you find in Brazilian life.

Of course one doesn't want to spend the rest of one's life in a place like Manaus and one morning I got a plane and flew down to Rio. The contrast was nice, too, and perhaps that's the other reason why one travels. In Rio I have several posh friends, and it was a change to put on a dinner jacket instead of sweaty khakis, to twirl a martini instead of a mug of warm cane spirit, and eat some swanky French cooking on a veranda looking over Rio's great bay instead of pushing down the rather monotonous food of Manaus in some fly-infested eating house. Yes, that's why one travels: for strangeness, and also for contrast. I remember being in Laos a few years ago. I wanted to see the Meo people of the mountains who are the great opium-growers of the world. They're a strange lot, the Meo. They live on the tops of the steep calcium mountains near the capital of Vientiane and to get up to them is the most dreadful job. The mountains just go straight up, it rains all the time and the clayey soil is as slippery as grease. I was taken by a Canadian missionary who was about the toughest young man I've ever met. He walked through the thick jungle to the foot of the mountain as though he were striding down a city street. Behind him I stumbled and panted. We had various streams to ford where he was as sure-footed as a goat while I just went under. When we got to the mountain of the opium growers he went up like a lift while I was up three steps, then down two. Coming down was even worse. The clay was interspersed with sharp rocks, and by the time I got to the bottom, most of the way on my backside, every scrap of clothing had been torn off my body. I made the return journey through the forest in my pyjamas.

When we got back to Vientiane after four days away I was pretty exhausted. I changed out of my pyjamas and took a plane straight on to Bangkok. Now Bangkok isn't a great centre of civilization but compared to anywhere in Laos it's like New York. I didn't have much money but I took a taxi from the airport to the most expensive hotel. I had just enough for a good dinner and a night's rest. I got straight into the kidney-shaped swimming pool and swam away my jungle aches. Then I dressed up as grandly as I could, had a couple of cocktails and a candle-lit dinner. The point of this rather childish wallowing was that it was an utter contrast to the jungle walk, the climb to the village and the two nights spent on the mud floor of an opium-grower's hut.

Strangeness and contrast; the two poles of the traveller's life. On the way from one pole to the other, there's another thing, perhaps the most precious of all. I'll risk sounding pretentious and call it the sense of wonder. After all life is literally wonderful, even if it does its best most of the time not to seem so. I got this feeling most strongly in East Africa a few years ago. I enjoy looking at wild animals. I don't feel the slightest drive to shoot them, that seems to me the act of a madman, and I don't even want to photograph them. After all there are plenty of pictures of wild animals in books. I just like looking at them, sort of storing them up in my head, and of course East Africa is absolutely the place for this. The famous game parks, such as the Serengeti and Ngorongoro Crater, are very fine; but my favourite is a much smaller crater called Ngordoto. It's situated at the foot of Mount Kilimanjaro, it's not very spectacular, just a couple of miles across and perhaps five hundred feet deep, but you get the most extraordinary feeling there. Not many tourists go to Ngordoto and on the day I went no one else was there at all. The animals are not very spectacular. I didn't see any lions or elephants but as I lay on the crater rim and looked down at its floor, rather as one might look into a pond, and saw the wildebeeste and impala and giraffes in their herds, I had this extraordinary feeling that I was the only man in the world, the first man as it were, who had walked through the forest and come to this crater and looked down and seen these creatures. That's what I mean by the sense of wonder that's sometimes brought into play when one travels. Indeed it's to feed it that one does travel and it's nice that even with approaching middle age the sense of wonder doesn't seem to have died or withered.

It's what you feel when you wake up in the morning on a boat in Penang harbour and see the East for the first time: you smell copra and see Chinese junks and hear the chatter of the coolies, and these things combine to produce an overwhelming sensation. Or it's what you feel when you're crossing Russia by train, travelling for days on end across that vast landscape, with the loudspeakers in all the carriages playing Mussorgsky and Borodin interminably, and looking out of the window you suddenly realize what the music is all about, how the Russian composers had written out of just such a feeling of emptiness and immensity. Then of course there are the various natural marvels, the things that are automatically supposed to produce the sense of wonder. In me they don't always. I shall never forget flying over the Himalayas but something like the Sahara is really a bit of a bore and I could never whip up much enthusiasm for the Bay of Naples. South America certainly has its share of natural marvels and I suppose the Amazon comes first. The trouble with the Amazon though is that it's really *too* big, you can't see it all at once, so that paradoxically it appears less grand than it is. The harbour at Salvador in Brazil is really much more exciting than the more famous one at Rio; the Iguassu Falls knock Niagara and the Victoria Falls into a cocked hat. And so on.

Still, for me, the natural marvels are not the main thing. I could manage without them. You can get the sense of wonder much better from the ordinary things in the extraordinary places: an afternoon in a slum village outside Rio; a visit to the market in La Paz where the Indian men wear top hats and their women bowlers; a look at the Japanese quarter in São Paulo where in the middle of the most Americanized city in South America you couldn't believe you weren't in a village in Japan. These are surprises and the important thing is to keep being surprised even if you've got to go to the ends of the earth. I hope I don't run out of earth. I'm not worried for the time being. I'm off again in a week or two.

2

The Worst Place in the World
[August 1965]

FLYING down to Rio in the VC-10 a few months ago, with the latest James Bond in one hand and a glass of champagne in the other, I wasn't disposed to agree with the gloomy fellow sitting beside me. He'd been asking what I was doing and so I told him the splendid menu I'd planned for myself in South America: first of all Rio, where the girls are; and then Salvador, the old capital of Brazil, with its fabulous Baroque churches; after that a trip from Buenos Aires up the River Paraguay, on an only half-serious hunt for Nazis in hiding; then up to Bolivia where the llamas are and the peasant women wear bowler hats; then down the Amazon back into Brazil to Manaus, which can't be reached by road or rail, but where Sarah Bernhardt performed in what is still the biggest opera house in the Western world; and on to French Guiana, that ghostly seldom-visited piece of France Overseas that's remembered only because of Devil's Island, once the most terrible penal colony in the world, which was where I wanted to go. But my gloomy neighbour didn't think any of these plans was a good idea, especially the French Guiana bit. 'That's the worst place in the world,' he said, and not very discouraged I went back to my champagne and James Bond.

Nor was I discouraged when I got to the worst place in the world a month or so later and found myself in Cayenne, the capital—a pretty, shabby copy in pastel colours of a French provincial town, executed mainly in corrugated iron. Driving from the airport one was suddenly in the Caribbean, and I'd been in Latin South America just long enough to enjoy the change for a few days. The plane back to Brazil was once a week so I had just the right amount of time to enjoy Negro languor instead of Latin laissez faire, to stumble through commonplaces with strangers in the sing-song nonsense of Petit-Nègre (the French Caribbean equivalent of Pidgin English), instead of my wretched Portuguese or Spanish, and to sit and sip a French apéritif and watch the tall Creole girls in their bright muslin dresses strolling through the sunlight with the grace of sailing ships. In other words one settled in nicely in Cayenne with no trouble at all. All afternoon on my first day I sat in the Place des Palmistes, lounging in a café with new friends, talking and watching the empty square and the Emperor palms, those superb trees that go two hundred feet straight up until at the top a tuft of leaves catches what they call in those parts the Traveller's Wind, a breeze that rarely reaches down into the sweaty streets.

So it was hot, and we sat still and waited for that marvellous hour that comes in tropical cities at sunset, when the world of the sun dies and the human world comes to life again. I picked up my bag and strolled across the Place in the dusk to my hotel. The Place des Palmistes is more like a piece of jungle than a city square and suddenly in front of me, across the path like a torpedo, shot an iguana as big as a small dog. Bats flapped about between the trees and anonymous things whistled or grunted in the bushes and I was quite glad to reach the hotel. There was nobody about except a big white-haired Negro who spoke English in a British Caribbean accent. 'You come across the grass, mister?' he said, pointing back to the way I'd come. 'You don't want to do that after dark, or bushmaster will find you.' I don't suppose there are many capitals where killer snakes roam the streets at night, but if you think you've just escaped them there's something rather exhilarating about the idea and so I remembered my gloomy friend on the plane cheerfully enough. Though I'd come to French Guiana for a gloomy enough reason myself I suppose: to have a look at what was left of Devil's Island. Why, I don't know. Partly, I suppose, because I like to placate the ghosts of my childhood and once upon a time Devil's Island (read about in magazines and boys' adventure books) was a place full of terror and strange excitement; partly because of course the idea of actually *going* to Devil's Island was fun. But how was I to get there? The penal colony was closed in 1947 but in its time it was a smear on the name of La Belle France and the French authorities in Guiana today don't encourage your interest in the subject. Devil's Island is one of three islands called (rather unfortunately) the Iles du Salut and they are about eight miles out to sea with shoals and difficult currents and sharks to avoid.

However I seem to be a lucky traveller, lucky at finding people to help me in strange places, and I was lucky again this time, or so I thought. I'd kept quiet about Devil's Island in the café in the square, feeling my way in case the idea wasn't popular, but now on an impulse I put my problem to the white-haired Negro. With a fine expansive gesture he produced an instant solution. He had a friend with a boat. The friend wasn't frightened of the sharks, of the difficult landing, or of the ghosts of dead convicts that are said to inhabit the Iles du Salut. All that was needed was money, more than I would have liked, but you only go to Devil's Island once in your life. We sealed the deal with a planter's punch, and then another, and after a great many more my Negro friend went off to fix the boat for the morning and I went to my room, an interminable journey along dark creaking corridors to a small cell with no lock on the door and no windows and a bed with dirty sheets. The only other furniture was a small rickety table with a glass ashtray on it. Previous guests had written French obscenities on the wallpaper. In the bathroom next door was the biggest spider I have ever seen, with a yellowish body like a poached egg and long hairy legs. I went to bed unwashed, listening to the hotel creaking around me, as if marauders were prowling the corridors. Thinking of the door without any lock and the gloomy man's advice about the worst place in the world, I put all my money and my passport in my shoe and put that under my pillow. Then I balanced the glass ashtray on the door handle and went to sleep. At what hour of the morning I don't know, I woke with jangling nerves to the crash of breaking glass. Uncomfortably aware that I had no pants on, I jumped out of bed, grabbed the bedside table by one leg as a weapon and switched the light on. Framed in the door was a sad figure, an elderly European dressed in rags with no shoes on, swaying and obviously drunk. He stared at me in a confused way, mumbled something and went out. I went back to bed but not to sleep. If this was the worst place in the world, I'd better have my wits about me.

In the morning my Negro friend came to drive me to the boat I'd hired and I told him about the ragged old man. 'Dat's the fellow Pellissier. He's a libéré,' and he explained that any criminal sentenced to the penal colony in the old days had to serve first his sentence in prison, and then serve the same time all over again as an ordinary inhabitant of French Guiana before he was allowed to return to France. These were the libérés, and when the penal colony was closed down and the prisoners sent back to France, a few of them elected to stay on in Guiana. There are a dozen or so left today, most of them little but beggars, drinking cheap rum and scavenging from dustbins, and my visitor of the night was one. By now we had arrived at the boat and it wasn't really a boat at all, I wasn't surprised to see, but something more like a canoe with a dilapidated outboard motor which took half an hour to start.

Off we went, and as we baled with a rusty baked-beans tin, my white-haired friend told me about the sharks. The Iles du Salut are small and rocky and there was nowhere to bury a convict when he died or was murdered by one of the others. So they used to take the body out in a boat and chuck it in the sea, to be dealt with by the sharks. When the bell tolled in the prison church to signal a funeral, the sharks would hear and poke their snouts above the waves, waiting for their dinner. Of course, this was just the sort of information I needed to hear as we lurched in our little boat into the troughs of waves far higher than ourselves, but gradually the islands came nearer, and after a couple of hours we landed on the Ile Royale, about a mile around and the biggest of the three islands. What a heavenly place, I thought, and not only because we'd escaped the sharks. Tall palms waved in a soft South Sea island sort of breeze; wild flowers grew everywhere; coconuts lay on the ground; and a lovely green parrot flew out of a tree. At first we saw no buildings. Then we came on the first of the prison barracks. The roof had fallen in, but everything else was as it had been. The bunks where the convicts had slept were piled to the ceiling like shelves; at the foot of each bunk was a leg iron secured to the wall; and these irons were always fastened before the convicts were left for the night. After nearly twenty years they're a bit rusty, but they'd still hold a human leg all right. Most of the scribbles on the walls had been washed away by the tropical rains, but in a sheltered corner I found one prisoner's farewell to the Iles du Salut: '*Jean Clouzot 16 Avril 1946. Mater Dolorosa Ora Pro Nobis*'.

We climbed up to the top of the island, and there was Devil's Island itself, a few hundred yards away, looking even more heavenly than Royale. The palms waved in the wind, and the surf crashed on the rocks. The sea was like green and blue marble, but the rocks make any landing almost impossible. Nobody ever escaped from Devil's Island, and there was no need for prison guards there. The prisoners were sent over from Royale on a sort of cableway that has long since collapsed, and once there they were left to their own devices. Devil's Island was mostly for political prisoners, and this was where Dreyfus lived alone in a hut for five years until he was proved innocent. We turned our backs on Devil's Island and walked through the palms and the wild orchids towards the church with its corrugated-iron spire. On the way we passed a brick and concrete structure raised above the ground. 'Madame Guillotine,' said my white-haired friend with a gesture, and we wandered on without a pause to the church. 'You will see paintings in church, very good,' he'd said, and here they were, not good at all but very strange. They were murals painted by one of the convicts who'd been a master forger in civilian life, and here he'd taken to painting religious subjects: with a difference. The faded scenes on the walls looked conventional enough at first: the Sermon on the Mount; the money-changers in the temple; the miracle of the loaves and fishes; until you saw that worked into each picture was a tragic prison motif. At the foot of the Cross on Calvary was a little pile of whips, manacles and hammers for breaking stone, emblems of the convict's servitude. Among the throng receiving the loaves and fishes was a man in the red-striped uniform of a convict who got nothing. The prodigal son was painted as a convict returning to the world outside. 'More pictures in Cayenne. I will take you to see,' said my guide, but for the time being I had seen enough and we went back to the boat, past more barracks and along the catwalk over the dreadful solitary confinement cells, sunk into the ground like graves. An iguana flicked his long tail among the palms, and we left the island to him, and puttered back through the alarming waves to Cayenne and a few stiff drinks.

It was pretty obvious that for some people anyway French Guiana had indeed been the worst place in the world. With the idea of cheering myself up the next morning I dropped into the local museum. I have a fondness for small museums, like the ones you find in English country towns, the sort of place with two small rooms at the back of the Town Hall, full of a clutter of stuffed birds and ships in bottles and faded photographs and old stamp collections. The small museum in Cayenne isn't a bit like this. The only stuffed object is a gigantic crocodile which completely fills the entrance hall. A label tells you that this horrible animal belonged to a former Prefect, who used to keep it tied up in his garden, rather as you might keep an Alsatian to frighten the neighbour's children away. Most of the rest of the museum is devoted to mementoes of the penal colony, lovingly preserved. The guillotine whose foundations I saw on Ile Royale is there, and somebody has smeared some red paint on the blade, or it may be blood for all I know. There are some plaster casts of the limbs of prisoners who were tortured by the guards. There is a series of scale models of the prisons, done with painstaking care by a devoted miniaturist, complete with lilliputian prisoners and warders, miniature barbed wire, and even a tiny guillotine that works.

I soon had enough of this, and went to pay a call I had been promising myself. Cayenne has only two restaurants, and one of them had seemed irresistible since I'd seen a poster at the airport advertising its charms. 'Musical afternoons and dinner parties at Restaurant Palm Beach,' it had said in English, 'exotic scenery and cheapest in town, table delicacies, cocktails, coffee and liqueurs of first choice, good cellar and faultless attendance.' A musical afternoon with faultless attendance sounded like a nice change, so I got hold of my Negro friend and his car. 'Sure I take you,' he said. 'That is Macheras' place. He is the man with the pictures,' and at first I didn't put two and two together. Out at the Restaurant Palm Beach I soon did. Macheras turned out to be another libéré, the only one who had made anything of his so-called freedom. The Palm Beach turned out to be a long room facing the sea. All along one side tall windows gave on to a dreamy beach, another South Seas affair with whispering palms and creaming surf. On the other side of the room hung the strangest paintings I'd ever seen. This was the forger again, the man who'd painted the murals in the church on Ile Royale. Eventually he'd become a libéré, and when Macheras started this restaurant, he'd commissioned his old friend to do the décor. The result was these paintings. They were a kind of stations of the damned, charting the whole progress of a convict's life in a sharply etched style that made you see he must have been a good forger. Here in paint were the convicts taking their last leave of France, here they were on board the transport ship shut up like animals in a huge cage, here disembarking in the cruel and beautiful Douanier Rousseau world of Guiana. Next they were in their cells, playing cards or fighting with knives or sunk in silent despair, or locked in grave-like solitary-confinement cells. Here they were working at tasks fit only for animals; or trying to escape in flimsy home-made canoes, and facing the penalty of recapture which was always death. Here they were making their last journey to feed the sharks.

Beneath these strange pictures presumably the haut-bourgeois of Cayenne enjoyed their musical afternoons. I asked for the man who had commissioned these pictures, and my Negro friend pointed him out, a gaunt elderly figure stretched in a deck-chair at the end of the room, crossing and uncrossing his legs, jerking his head, restlessly brushing his face with his hand. 'Do not try and speak with him,' my friend said. 'He is very nervous,' and suddenly I found I didn't really want to. He was the only person in the room who knew what those pictures were about, and when I looked at them again, those textbook illustrations of human misery, I wasn't sure I wanted to know any more. So we went away, we left him there, with his memories written on his walls, and later from the beach through the tall windows I caught a last sight of him, this libéré with no freedom from his past, crossing and uncrossing his legs, restlessly brushing his face with his hand, an angry ghost haunting his own house.

3
The Smugglers' Express
[August 1965]

WHEN I left Reyes in Bolivia at seven in the morning I was stone-cold sober; when I arrived at La Paz an hour later I had a hangover. I'd gone to Reyes from Rurenabaque on a pony along the forest path because that's the way Colonel Fawcett went on his first Bolivian expedition sixty years ago. Those were the days of the great Amazon rubber boom when slave merchants used to raid the Indian villages and jaguars roamed the jungle. The jaguars are still there they say but I didn't see any as I trotted painfully along. But the villages are certainly still there, clusters of wretched huts as squalid as I've seen anywhere, so I wasn't sorry after two days to get to Reyes and pick up a lift there to La Paz on the meat plane. Bolivia is a weird country, half of it jungle and fertile lowlands where hardly anybody lives, and the other half a high plateau like Tibet where most of the people are, although it's the most unsuitable place in the country for them to be. The two parts are divided by the terrific wall of the Andes and the only sensible way to get from one to the other is by plane. The local airline flies a not very serious schedule, so I was lucky to pick up the old B-24 that flies fresh meat from the lowland ranches to the capital.

There the carcasses were, piled like sacks down both sides of the windowless tube of the fuselage, and even at that hour, in the chill of early morning, they didn't smell as fresh as all that. The young American pilot who shovelled me in among the dead animals apologized for there being no oxygen except in the cockpit and gave me a polythene bag to be sick in. At the last moment another passenger was tipped in: a scrubby little old man in a dirty duck suit with the coat tied up with string. On his shoulder sat a very small monkey. There in the drumming hold we sat, all three of us, in the light of one weak bulb, while the great red sides of meat shifted creepily as the plane bumped in the air pockets. I tried out my Spanish on the little old man but he was too busy looking after the monkey, which was being sick. I stared at the carcasses apparently coming to life and wished I could see the beautiful Andes below. By the time we got to La Paz I had a hangover headache and when I got out of the plane I found I was staggering. I was relieved to see that the newly arrived passengers on some all-inclusive American tour were staggering too, blue-haired ladies and paunchy retired businessmen tottering about the customs lounge like people at sea in a storm. This was all because La Paz is the highest capital in the world, and the airport is even higher, perched among the Andes at over 13,000 feet. The runway is the longest in the world too and the planes charge along it for what seems like miles, struggling for lift in the thin air. A small hazard is the risk of hitting a llama, and I was almost brought out of my hangover state by the pleasure of seeing these animals for the first time outside the zoo, strolling with superior self-possession among the passengers waiting for taxis. The llamas seemed to prove that one really was in Bolivia, and so did the next splendid experience: seeing my first Bolivian Indian peasant woman. Are the traveller's tales true? Do these women really wear bowler hats above their rough blankets and shawls? I can report that they do.

Down to the city of La Paz, then, a descent of a couple of thousand feet to the bottom of a bowl surrounded by snowy mountains in a twenty-year-old taxi held together by wire and rope. I suppose La Paz must be one of the most attractive capitals in South America, with the lovely Spanish colonial houses climbing up steep streets to the Babylonian colour and confusion of the Indian quarters on the heights. Getting up the stairs in the hotel turned one blue in the face but I forgot my headache when I saw the splendid scene from my balcony. Today was May Day, Labour Day, a great day for Bolivians, and just as much fun for a visitor. The streets were crammed with people; processions, banners and bands playing. The banners were the usual stuff: 'Go Home, Yanqui' and such-like expressions of Fidelismo. The bands were another matter: beribboned and bemedalled, with brass shining, they were playing the 'Stars and Stripes' and the 'Marseillaise' exclusively, for their stirring qualities more than their politics presumably. Although committed to such serious ideals the marchers were in a cheerful mood, walking along drinking beer out of the bottle and singing different songs from the ones the bands were playing. The whole May Day procession was led by the Minister of Labour. As Bolivia has a military government, he is a colonel, and he marched along in full comic-opera style uniform under a banner which in translation read 'Down with the Military Boot'. All this was a very heady experience and like most visitors to La Paz I had to retire to my bed in the middle of the afternoon, feeling as if I'd been up for days.

When I regained consciousness that evening a gigantic neon sign of a bed-pan, advertising a chemist shop, had gone on opposite my hotel window. Next to this was an equally large picture of the President, lit up round the edges with coloured bulbs. How long he was going to be President was a matter of debate. Since he took the job over last year, after Bolivia's 179th revolution in the country's 140 years of existence, the President has survived four attempts on his life, most of them organized by himself, or so people said. Perhaps that's why the assassins always missed, except the last time, when the President was wounded in the backside while driving along in his jeep. Though the rumour about that was that he'd sat on the safety catch of his own revolver. Now revolution was brewing again, or so people said. You could only reach La Paz by air because the peasants were blockading the roads. The tin-miners were reported to be planning a rising. The Americans were rumoured to be stepping up aid to the government. Castro himself was said to be taking an interest in developments. The Chinese (the reports are getting fainter now) were flying in arms. . . .

I was in Bolivia as a correspondent for a London paper, trying to find out what was really going on, and so for my first few days in La Paz I diligently made the round of embassies, ministries, newspaper offices and bars. At the end of the week I hadn't the faintest idea what had happened or was going to happen and I'd come to the conclusion that the Bolivians didn't know either. This is a country where the politicians wake up in the morning and decide then what they are going to do that day. And this isn't because they take their job lightly. On the contrary, the Bolivian is a completely political animal. Nobody ever talks about anything else. In a country of four million people, most of them illiterate, there are seventeen political parties and numerous splinter groups. Indeed you could say that every thinking Bolivian is a separate political party on his own. Even the crosswords in the newspapers (which are called Boliviograms) require a very detailed knowledge of the political situation there. In the end I gave up all hope of understanding their current affairs and returned to the more congenial study of Bolivian pleasures.

This is the poorest country in South America, and the Bolivians take their pleasures rough. Bolivian drinking was a new experience. For the visitor the effects are rather rapid, because of the altitude, but this doesn't seem to worry the locals. The poorer ones take their drink pretty well neat, by which I mean they buy it as neat alcohol, sold in special shops in tins like the cans you buy a pint of oil in. You go into the alcohol shop and buy one of these tins, knock a couple of holes in it with a nail, and drink the stuff unadulterated until you fall down. The Bolivians' other pleasures are just as extreme. Bolivia is the home of the coca plant, from which cocaine is made, and you can buy the coca leaves all over town. They are small heart-shaped green leaves, and if you chew a sackful of them, you go quietly off your head. I had a go at this, but it was more like chewing the front lawn than having a wicked adventure, and I gave up. The Bolivians are made of sterner stuff and in the steep streets of La Paz you occasionally come across a fellow who's unhinged himself, sitting on the ground and mumbling.

Like all South Americans, Bolivians are mad about sport, and especially soccer, always known as 'futbol'. They take their futbol almost as seriously as their politics. The most terrific fight I've seen for years was between two supporters of rival clubs in La Paz, and it wasn't even at a match, but in the street. I thought somebody would be killed. The third thing a Bolivian will fight about, after politics and football, is a woman. I went prowling round the night clubs of La Paz, but it was hours before I could get into one, because I didn't have a woman with me. The reasoning is that if you haven't got a woman you'll try and pinch somebody else's, and in the resulting fight the joint will be wrecked. In the only place that would let me in I couldn't have stolen a woman if I'd tried, because I couldn't see one. The place was so dark that the management had painted phosphorescent rings round the glasses so you could find your way to your drink.

I was beginning to long for the softer airs of Brazil, but the altitude in La Paz seems to breed a strange lassitude and I don't know when I would have got moving if it hadn't been for the march of the furious women. La Paz is a town of processions and meetings, people are always protesting about something and you stop noticing them. But I couldn't help opening my eyes at this strident procession of angry, ragged peasant women marching down the main street, beating saucepans and shouting abuse against the government. When I asked who they were someone said this was the Smugglers' Union. A lot of Bolivians in the lowlands make their living by smuggling cocaine and rubber across the border into Brazil, and smuggling various luxuries like tinned goods into Bolivia which Bolivia doesn't manufacture. A lot of this smuggling is winked at, but apparently border controls had been tightened up lately and these ladies were protesting at this iniquitous interference of the law, and public opinion was with them. I understand they got their way in the end and I'm glad because they did me a good turn, since asking about this smuggling of theirs led me to hear of the Smugglers' Express. This is the train that carries the smugglers between Santa Cruz in eastern Bolivia and Corumba in Brazil, where 'scarcely a week ever passes without fatal gunplay between the populace'—according to Colonel Fawcett in 1909. No doubt things have changed, I thought, and this seemed a nice way to get back into Brazil, so I got a plane and flew down to Santa Cruz to pick up the Smugglers' Express.

It was a once-a-week train, so I had a couple of days to look at Santa Cruz. It's the nearest to a Wild West town I've been in, down to hitching posts for horses in front of bars with wooden verandas and swinging half-doors. If the citizens didn't let off their guns, they certainly carried them around. It was all rather exhilarating, and when the train arrived that was better still. You remember the Marx Brothers film about the Wild West when the Brothers are escaping by train from the Red Indians and they run out of wood for the locomotive so they begin chopping the train up? Well, the carriages of the Smugglers' Express looked as if they'd had the same treatment. Where there were seats or wooden window blinds, half of these had been chopped up for firewood, not for the engine but to make fires in the carriages themselves for passengers to cook on. On the floor of each carriage there were large scorched patches where the fires had been. Most of the carriages had never had seats: they were simply cattle trucks, some with a roof and some without—these were the second class. The first class were the coaches with the scorched floors. The engine was a magnificent relic of the last century which rained out red-hot ash from underneath. As a result most of the wooden sleepers on the line had been singed at some time, and some were burned away altogether. I don't know how the rails kept in a straight line. At night it was a cheerful sight to see from the last coach the sleepers glowing in the darkness sometimes for miles behind. On this self-consuming railroad caution is the keynote, and the journey from Santa Cruz to Corumba, 400-odd miles, takes forty-eight hours.

What did we do all that time, the smugglers and I? My Spanish is not very good, but I know enough to play poker, and we played for two days and nights almost without stopping. The stakes were tiny, and I won about a pound in that time. They didn't seem to be very successful smugglers. Most of them were men with stubbly faces and bad-tempered expressions and not the gusty ladies who'd been marching in La Paz. In fact I couldn't see what these people were smuggling and the matter was not discussed, as far as I could understand. I suppose cocaine doesn't take up much room. I began to be rather bored with the whole business.

We went on playing poker, and the train went on for ever across an endless plain, with nothing to see but bush and the not quite parallel rails stretching away ahead and behind. Occasionally someone saw an animal or bird, or thought he saw one, and blazed away with a revolver or shot-gun out of the side of the carriage. But nobody hit anything. We stopped at featureless halts next to villages, and ragged women came out and sold us undrinkable coffee. It was far too hot, and I was thoroughly sick of poker and my disappointingly tame smuggler friends. As so often, wandering around the world, I wondered what I was doing in this slow and smelly train, why I was eating this filthy food that was giving me a pain, sleeping on a hard wooden floor, playing poker with these dismal crooks, travelling from one dreary place to another doubtless as dreary, both of them thousands of miles from home; as I say, I wondered what on earth I was doing there, but I knew at the same time I wouldn't be anywhere else.

4
The New People
[August 1965]

I was recently in Brazil for six weeks, travelling all over the country, from the big cities like Rio and São Paulo and Brasilia to the desolate North-East and the Amazon and the jungles of the Matto Grosso; yet what I've come back with isn't so much an impression of the huge, marvellous country, bigger and more varied than the continental United States, but an impression rather of the people, themselves as varied as the country, all of them very definitely different from people elsewhere and different in the same way. In the other countries I went to in South America, I met Argentinians and Uruguayans and Bolivians but never felt there was anything as special about them as the Brazilians. In most of South America the influence of Europe is still very strong. Argentinians are not so much Argentinians as Spaniards or Germans or British living in the Argentine. I know this isn't what they think of themselves but as soon as you get to Brazil you see that this is in fact so—because the Brazilians are quite distinctly Brazilian in the way that we in Europe are British or French or Dutch or whatever we are. In Brazil, then, I felt I was meeting a new kind of man, a very interesting kind, and one moreover to give one an added interest in and hope for the future. This is because of all the countries in the world today Brazil is easily the most heterogeneous. It's a unique porridge of races and nationalities —Negroes from Africa, Portuguese and Italians and Germans from Europe, Japanese and Chinese and Russians from Asia—and the fact they have become welded together in the way they have is the most hopeful thing I've seen for years.

Last year I went to Iceland and was excited by what I found. Here at last seemed to be the Good Society, where men were equal and decent and as happy as the human condition allows, but my pleasure was limited by what I realized were the limits of the enterprise. In a country isolated from the world, with a population of a couple of hundred thousand, a country that was more of a family, the Good Society was possible perhaps. In anywhere larger and more complex it has not survived for long. Now Brazil and the Brazilians, the New People of South America, have revived the hope that we may be able to live in something less squalid than the state we find ourselves in today.

What strikes everybody on their first day in Brazil is that this really is a democracy. It's not that everybody is equal. Brazil is a country with great extremes of rich and poor, where democratic institutions flourish, but in the rich manure of corruption. What's important about the Brazilians is that they *feel* equal. A splendid place to watch this going on is on the famous beach in the suburb of Rio called Copacabana. This is real democracy. The beach itself, so absurdly glamourized in travel advertisements, is in fact not much of a beach. If you lie on it you get bitten by sand flies. Across the middle of it flows a trail of sewage. If you get off the beach and into the water you run a fair risk of drowning in the dangerous currents. As for the people there they are not, of course, the bronzed Apollos and Venuses of the travel posters but a very ordinary, though quite extraordinarily mixed, cross-section of Latin humanity. Most of them are indeed very brown to start with. That doesn't matter because here astonishingly is a country where colour doesn't exist. People in Brazil don't care what colour you are. The last beauty queen at Copacabana was a blonde of German extraction; the previous one was a Negress. On the beach any colour can talk to any other; any class to any other; anybody to anybody. The most exciting thing for the newly arrived visitor is that none of the normal checks which hold up human contact seem to exist in Brazil. If you speak to a strange woman she doesn't immediately assume you want to pick her up, or if she does she feels quite capable of dealing with the situation. If you speak to a strange man he doesn't think you're trying to get something out of him, or if he does he knows perfectly well that it's up to him whether you succeed or not. In other words, because people think well of themselves, they are liable to think well (or at least, tolerantly) of others. To some degree these qualities are true of all South Americans, though I think the remark of an Argentine writer applies even more to the Brazilians than to his own countrymen. 'We behave,' he said, 'as if each of us were unique and as if each of us were alone,' which seems to me to be a pretty good description of a mature man.

Now I know it is easy to sentimentalize anything to do with equality, democracy and so on. I know the situation isn't perfect: how could it be? There is colour prejudice in Brazil, but very little, and much of it because of foreign and especially American influence. Much of it is really a form of money snobbery. Because the Negroes came to Brazil from West Africa in the first place as slaves, there are bound to be traces of servitude in their psychology, and it's inevitable in a country with an every-man-for-himself economy that up to now people of predominantly Negro stock should for the most part be located in the lower sector of that economy. After all, if you start at the bottom you've got further to climb. But I don't see how there can ever be any serious colour prejudice in Brazil, for the simple fact that almost everyone there *is* coloured. The first time you walk down a street in Rio, or ride on a bus, your reaction is that there's not a white person in the place. Everybody is a kind of nondescript coffee-and-cream colour. I suppose it's more popular to be white, but even the people who say they are white, aren't. One patrician gentleman who made some mildly anti-black remark to me was himself of a complexion that would give him some trouble if he was trying to rent a room in London today. A nice example of the colour situation in Brazil was shown me by a young Brazilian diplomat. Over cocktails in his expensive house I asked him about this colour business. He beckoned to me to follow him into his children's bedroom. There they lay side by side in their cots, three sons by the same mother. One was very brown, one as blond as a Scandinavian, and one sort of in between. That settled the matter as far as I was concerned.

Quite as agreeable as the lack of racial tension is the general toleration of nationality. Or perhaps one should put it another way: that Brazil has a surprising capacity to make Brazilians out of the people who come there. I should think about half the population of 75 million or so must be at the most only second-generation Brazilians, yet assimilation has been almost complete. No strong measures are used to bring this about either. Portuguese is taught in all the schools, of course, but other languages are taught as well. People are not discouraged from living with their own national groups, and in fact there are some astonishing communities, especially in São Paulo state. I have been to a village where you could have sworn you were in Japan, and a town where you were almost certainly in the Tyrol except for the temperature of 100 degrees. Yet the people concerned were speaking Portuguese as well as German and Japanese, and certainly considered themselves Brazilian. There is a large number of Italians, and if distinctions can be made at all, they seem to have made the transfer most completely. There are White Russians, and Greeks, and Chinese, and Syrians and Lebanese, and all of them have more or less completely transferred their loyalties. Brazil is full of small bizarre experiences in this area that I suppose in a better world would not be surprising at all.

A concomitant of this easygoing attitude to race and nationality is a tolerance of personal conduct amounting to licence. I find this exhilarating, though I suppose some people wouldn't. I am against rules for behaviour, providing cruelty to individuals is not involved. Almost anything goes in Brazil, and I won't say short of murder, because you can get away with that, too. Indeed I met my first murderer in Salvador. He'd shot his wife's lover, and then given himself up to the police. Everybody was very embarrassed, and it was thought expedient to shut him away in the city gaol for a month or so. While he was there, scores of people came to congratulate him on his manly action. After a while, charges were quietly dropped, or rather never preferred, and he returned home. He is a well-off man of position, and of course this helped, but in any case a few months is all he would have got. There is no death penalty in Brazil. In sexual matters there is almost total permissiveness, as long as you show a decent discretion. Sex is regarded as fun, which I hope to God is sensible enough. As a result, there is practically no sexual crime in this huge and undisciplined country.

Permissiveness is fairly total in other areas of life too. The business ethics of Brazil would raise eyebrows here, but I can't see that they're so dreadful. Corruption is fairly general. It's impossible, for instance, for an individual to do business with a government department without making use of a fixer, a *despachente* as he's called, a middle man who has contacts and will place them at your disposal for a percentage. What's wrong with this? He's only doing his job, and saving you the bother of doing it. Brazilians are very pragmatic people. They like to do what works, not what is thought proper. The whole inflation scandal is an interesting example of this. When that extraordinary man Jucelino Kubitschek, President of Brazil in the late 'fifties, decided the time had come to yank his country violently into the present, he found he was short of money. He wanted to build the new capital of Brasilia, to build factories, dams and roads, to start huge electrification schemes, and so on. He was short of money, so he decided on the extraordinary and desperate policy of making money, literally printing money without regard to the possibility, indeed the certainty, of creating an inflationary spiral. The cost of living shot up, and the result was to put the poorer and salaried people of Brazil through financial hell for ten years. They are only getting out of it now. But Kubitschek knew perfectly well that foreign aid would pay his debts in the end, and when the end threatened the Americans came up trumps. Today Brazil owes a lot of money, but Brasilia has been built, the factories, dams and roads have been built, Brazil no longer has to import anything very much, and the country of the future looks now as if it may have a future. Kubitschek himself is not allowed to stand for president now, by decree of the present American-backed military government, but if he did everybody in Brazil agrees he would get in. This capacity for doing what works, however unconventional it is, is at the heart of the Brazilian experience. They have a name for it: *jeto* they call it. The word means something like knack. They are the people with the knack; most of all, I would say, with the knack of living.

5
On the River Sea
[August 1965]

THERE are so many things I've never done that I meant to do, like writing a novel or learning to fly or going to Tibet, that it was nice to find myself a few months ago *doing* something that I'd meant to do for thirty years: taking a slow boat up the Amazon. Ever since I'd measured that long, snaky river that nearly cuts South America in half with a pair of calipers in the school atlas—the only river in the atlas wide enough to have blue water in it (the others were just wiggly lines)—ever since I was in short pants, I've had my eye on the Amazon; and so when I found myself at the end of last March in Belem at the mouth of the river, I felt pretty good. I wasn't going to do anything especially adventurous: just take a week's journey in a small trading steamer up as far as Manaus, the decaying capital of the Brazilian state of Amazonas, which is nearly a thousand miles upstream. But when I saw the river from the plane coming into Belem, I had a moment of disappointment. What did the geography books say? The Amazon is supposed to be 150 miles wide at the mouth, and here from the plane I could easily see what seemed to be the other bank. The explanation was that I was looking at one of thousands of islands in the river. This one was actually as big as Sunderland I found out afterwards. The Amazon isn't just one stream and only slowly does the immensity of the river grow on you. Not for nothing does Amazon mean the River Sea. I didn't want to do my trip on a liner, though big ships do go up to Manaus, and ships of a couple of thousand tons even up to Iquitos in Peru, which is 2,000 miles upstream and well over half-way across the whole continent.

The trouble is these ships have time to make, bulk cargoes and passengers to carry into the hinterland, whereas I wanted to idle my way across the fringes of the river and see a little of the people and the strange creatures that live there. So it was lucky I heard of the S.S. *João Gonçalves*, one of the tiny fussy steamers that serve the small villages along the great stream. She was sailing that night and I hurried off to look for her. Apparently there was no shipping agent, or anything like that: you simply went on board and bought a ticket from the captain, who owned the boat and operated her as a sort of long-distance river bus. In Belem it rains every afternoon punctually at three and again just after sunset, so I found myself tramping in the dark in the warm rain from one end of the docks to the other, tripping over hawsers and watching anxiously for the huge rats that leaped around in the shadows like rabbits. There was no sign of the *João Gonçalves*. I walked back along the wharves, feeling a bit depressed at missing the boat. At the dock gates the watchman challenged me and I explained why I was there. Silently he pointed at an empty space on the quayside nearby, and then, seeing I didn't understand, came out of his little box into the rain and guided me to the spot. There was the *João Gonçalves*, all couple-of-hundred-odd tons of her, with only her crooked smokestack showing a little above the wharfside. A couple of petrol lamps on her deck gave a dim view of rusting plates, peeling paint, and broken railings. The glass was broken in the window of the wheelhouse. She had a lifeboat, but not attached to its davits. There was no way down to the little boat except to jump. I nearly landed on the Captain, and he gave me a friendly grin. Yes, indeed, he'd carry me to Manaus, a thousand miles with a cabin to myself and full board for the equivalent of seven pounds. He was leaving in half an hour. Would I have a *cafezinho* (a tiny cup of very strong, very sweet Brazilian coffee) or perhaps a glass of *cachassa* (a fierce Brazilian spirit made from sugar cane)?

We had a glass or two and I tried not to worry about the pronounced list of the deck, the dilapidated air of the ship, and the other passengers and crew, to whom the Captain introduced me. There was a jolly little man in a cowboy shirt, who carried a pistol at his hip; a mulatto girl who would have been pretty if she'd had any teeth; a very fat man whose paunch bulged over the khaki shorts that were all he had on; a couple of other jolly mulattos who were full of the cane spirit; and several anonymous bustling Negroes who were tying down the cargo and generally making ready. And there was the pilot, a strikingly handsome mulatto with a supercilious air who was responsible for getting us up the river. In the three thousand odd miles of the navigable Amazon, and in all its tributaries, there is only one navigation light, on an island off Belem, and that, I am told, is festooned with wrecks, presumably because navigators can't believe their eyes. In the Amazon there are thousands of deserted islands; thousands more of the even more dangerous floating islands, that are never in the same place two trips running; and there are the sandbanks that move constantly. The river is pretty dark because most nights are cloudy (by now we had left the harbour, and I was beginning to see all this), and most vessels (including our own, I saw) don't carry lights. Yet when the lights of Belem disappeared astern, we didn't slacken speed, but drove on all night into the blackness. For hours I stood staring into the dark from the pilot's side, as he gave small sharp monosyllabic commands to the helmsman. At times the blackness was so vast and empty that one might have been blind; other times I caught a hint of looming vegetation, and once, at about four in the morning, we got entangled at a particularly narrow bend in the channel, caught up in some mangrove swamp, and all the passengers woke up and barracked the Negro crew as they pushed with boathooks and baulks of timber. This was the Amazon jungle, and you could smell it like the breath of an animal in the dark, and when the engine stopped and it was silent you could hear strange frantic screams and whistling sounds and scrabblings. But the pilot never made another mistake, and I climbed into my bunk and slept, after smearing cane spirit over my face like shaving lotion to keep the mosquitoes away.

In the morning I had my first sight of the Amazon jungle, of its excitement and feeling of threat, and also its disappointments. Rather naïvely, I'd hoped to see all the strange creatures of the river, anacondas and alligators, and so forth, but of course a boat with an engine and a propeller roughs up the water, and the animals retreat to the side streams. The day began well with a lovely flight of parakeets sailing overhead while we were eating our breakfast, and ended well with macaws above and a toucan in a tree looking as if he needed a glass of stout, and a flock of gibbons swinging through the forest beside us. Anacondas, however, there wasn't a chance of seeing, and by the way they don't attack people and they are never as long as the travellers' tales say; alligators I only saw later, on a side expedition from Manaus, and very nasty they were: of all animals surely the hardest to like. Some of the nastiest creatures, of course, were *in* the river, as we'd soon have found out if the pilot made any mistakes. The least favourite fish among the river dwellers is something called the candiru, which is about the size of a silver-fish and likes to swim into the bodily orifices of humans. It's got spines shaped like an arrow-head, so once in it can't get out. Getting it out is a matter of surgery. Next on the black-list is the famous piranha, which goes mad at the smell of blood. Even a cut on the finger is enough to attract these monsters from a hundred yards, and they can strip the flesh off a man in two minutes with their razor teeth. The horrors of the Amazon fauna are, in fact, pretty spectacular. A casual traveller like myself would be unlucky if he came up against one of these creatures, but they're not fairy stories, and lots of river people die every year from snakebite, for example. The sucurucu or bushmaster, for instance, is just about the only snake with whom snake serum is useless, for the simple reason that he delivers such a massive dose that it's physically impossible to get enough serum into the victim in time to save him. Scorpions and tarantulas claim other victims and at Santarem along the Amazon I saw the biggest scorpion I've ever seen. I wanted to put a ring of fire round him and see if he would sting himself to death, as in the legend, but to tell the truth I was frightened to try: I'd heard how quickly they can move. Legend has more to do with our terror of these creepy creatures than reality I think. Vampire bats abound along the Amazon, but I'm told their bite is harmless though messy, and there's said to be a sort of giant catfish called the piraiba which can swallow a man, but I can't believe this has ever happened. And there are plenty of much more sympathetic creatures in and around the Amazon. In Manaus I saw a kinkaju and a most endearing sloth, hanging on to the arm of a man walking along the street; the river is full of turtles, and they make excellent steaks; and although I can't claim to have seen a manatee, or mermaid, they are found in the Amazon, and I did see a dolphin, near Prainha, about four hundred miles from the sea.

If the animals were diverting, the human beings weren't less so. You can get very fond of people you're only going to be with for a few days and never see again, as with my companions of the *João Gonçalves*. The Captain to start with was an ample man. Unlike most men in such great positions, he was always available for conversation, and never did any captaining at all. That he left to the handsome supercilious pilot and his remarkable sixth sense. The Captain wore a captain's peaked cap and when we called at the larger villages he would put on a clean shirt, or at any rate a shirt, and as far as the pilot and crew were concerned, he kept a dignified distance. But he put himself generously at the disposal of the passengers, especially the mulatto girl with no teeth and myself. I got the impression she was resisting his advances, which was perhaps why he had time left for drinking with me. She was an amazing girl. At least six foot six and built like a fast bowler, she had a great mass of black hair that would have been beautiful if she'd ever washed it, a handsome face and a marvellous figure, and a mouth that was lovely until she opened it and revealed her only two visible teeth, the eye-teeth I think they're called, two fangs at the corners of her mouth. She was a sort of Tarzan woman, and I vaguely resented even her mild interest in the Captain. He was generous with his *cachassa*; and all of us told our life stories to each other for five days until we got to Santarem, roughly about two-thirds of the way up to Manaus, when I lost patience with our snail's progress and set myself down.

Santarem wasn't a bad place to spend a day waiting for a plane to Manaus. First of all, it's the smuggling centre of the Amazon, with all sorts of stuff coming in by contraband boat or plane from the Guianas. These days, contraband is liable to be very boring, things like transistor radios and motor scooters, but you could buy whisky in Santarem at fifteen bob a bottle, and cocaine and heroin if that's what you wanted. In Santarem I met some pleasant people. I spent a splendid afternoon with a man called Lee who was descended from General Robert E. Lee of the South in the American Civil War. In the 1870s several hundred of the defeated Southerners settled along the Amazon. Pleasantly piquant was the fact of Mr. Lee being at least three-quarters black. I'd always wanted to come to Santarem because this was the place where the great Henry Wickham stole half a dozen rubber-tree seedlings which he took back to Kew

Gardens in the late nineteenth century. This killed the Brazilian rubber boom, because afterwards they were transplanted in Malaya.

Above all, I remember Santarem for meeting M. Thomas, as French as the name indicates. He was the man who told me a lot about the anacondas, the nasty candiru fish and the snakes, who'd been all over South America with no money and no reason except he wanted to have adventures and be able to talk about them. He drank beer after beer at my willing expense at the Palace Hotel in Santarem and spun me yarn after yarn which I would have liked to believe. I tried to be sceptical but Thomas told a good story. He was talking about taking risks. 'Well, of course, I believe every man has, oh, not nine like a cat but thirteen lives, and many of these lives I have spent.' He meant in struggles with anacondas and so on. 'How many?' I asked. 'Oh, I have spent perhaps nine, maybe ten lives.' 'What happens when you've spent twelve?' I wondered, expecting him to answer that he'd be sensible and settle down. 'No, no,' he said, 'then I wait for the next time, and that time I die.'

6
The Day of the Radishes
[February 1966]

I SAT in the main square of Oaxaca and watched the world go by. It was one of those perfect Mexican winter mornings, just warm enough under a wide blue flawless sky. I sat and watched the mulattos go by in their sombreros and the Indian women in their brightly woven skirts with babies on their backs, and felt entirely content to be here in Oaxaca two days before Christmas. It was early in the day for a tequila, but I thought I would have one anyway. 'Mozo,' I called, and a cheerful Indian waiter came running, a dumpy little man with the hair growing low on his forehead like a gorilla: very typically a member of the Zapotec tribe that live around Oaxaca. He brought the tequila, and I went through the agreeable ritual I had learned: to stretch the thumb and first finger of the left hand wide apart; to sprinkle the web of skin there finely with salt, then to toss the salt into my mouth (it's very vulgar to lick it off), quickly lower the tequila in one gulp and finally, before the taste either of the salt or the tequila had time to establish themselves, to bite deeply into the slice of lime that comes with the drink. The resulting taste is a sort of sweet and sour, tremendously pleasant, so much so that you don't notice the burning sensation as the tequila goes down and indeed with the taste of lime you don't really feel you've had an alcoholic drink at all: not until later. Then you realize you've been drinking a really rather peculiar drink.

I had another one, and the morning seemed more perfect than ever. The square was full of people, the citizens of Oaxaca and a few tourists and a lot of Zapotecs in from the countryside by bus or mule, because today was a great day, the Day of the Radishes, *Dia de los Rabanos*, part of the elaborate Christmas festivities of Oaxaca. Oaxaca is fairly far south in Mexico, only the more energetic of the swarms of American tourists get this far, and the local customs haven't got too corrupted. The ten days before Christmas is a great time in Oaxaca, all one long festival really, with the Day of the Radishes as the high-spot. During the day the town would fill with people, and the famous market of Oaxaca would be extra busy. That was where the people everywhere were on their way to. But I found the square a pleasant enough place to be for the time being.

Like all of Oaxaca it had a strange greeny sort of look, because most of the buildings in the town are made of an olive-coloured stone that seems to hold the clear light and give it out in a kind of glow. Walking through the streets from the station had been eerie: it was like walking under water in some kind of grotto. I'd seen where the taxis with tourists were heading, and headed elsewhere myself to find a cheaper hotel. Occasionally one is lucky, and in the Hotel Plaza I paid the equivalent of five shillings for just the kind of room I like, a spotless whitewashed cell like a monk's with nothing in it but a bed, a chair and table, and a washbasin. A few days before in another cheap hotel at Villahermosa I had found a vulture sitting in the washbasin, but there was nothing to disturb the harmony of my new quarters. The bed was inviting, but the trouble about travel I find is that you never get any sleep. How can one arrive in a strange town, with the streets full of interesting-looking people doing unfamiliar things, and go straight to bed? So out I went into the square, and drank a tequila to wake myself up. The square was greener even than the streets because of the laurel trees. In the middle was a delightful bandstand with curly ironwork in Second Empire style. On one side was one of those vast churches, so out of proportion to their surroundings, that you see everywhere in Mexico. I made my way across and went in.

I'd come to Mexico, among other reasons, to get away from Christmas, but I should have known better. Still, at least Christmas in Mexico is something much more than the commercialized drinking party it has become in England. Inside the church was just as big, with that overweight of decoration that makes Catholic churches in southern countries so stifling; but this time the decoration had been done by local Indian artists of real talent, and the blaze of gold and jewellery wasn't offensive, the Virgin looked like a virgin and not a painted doll, and the Christmas scenes of the manger and the wise men were moving in an unusual formalized way. But even more moving were the dozens of people, mostly Indians in from the country I guessed. They worshipped not only at the altar but everywhere in the church, before each saint, before each relic, sometimes it seemed before just a blank wall. The Virgin was fenced off to protect her from the crowds, but there was a sort of stand-in Virgin to one side, and here the devotees waited in turn to stroke her hair or face or touch her robe. I saw one woman with a baby touch the robe with an unlighted candle and then with the candle she stroked the skin of her baby all over, even under the baby's clothes. People say Christianity has had little real success among the Indians in South America, but after that morning in the church at Oaxaca I begin to wonder.

I came out into the sunlit square and made for the market. This is practically the biggest market in Latin America, and today was the biggest market day of the year. Oaxaca as I said is relatively unspoiled, but nowhere I know in the world is really unspoiled, and the first rows of stalls were a disappointment, with wheedling Indians bargaining to sell all the tedious debris of our so-called civilization: plastic combs, and thermos flasks, and dried-out tubes of toothpaste, and transistor radios; but as I went deeper into the market, things got better. This is an area of Mexico famous for its potters, and there were marvellously good things done in a kind of grey clay: urns and bowls and cooking pots and mugs, but also surprising things for pottery like bells and little tables and delightful children's whistles shaped like donkeys, with the blow-hole under the donkey's tail. Then there were toys made from papier mâché: little bears and donkeys and jaguars and crocodiles, all of them full of character and, this is the point, different from each other, not stamped out of some wretched plastic mould.

Everything in this toy department of the market seemed to be made out of something else. There were birds made from flower petals, tiny fruits made from marzipan, and fruit like apples carved into the shape of animals. Everything was very small, reminding one how universal is this strange human need to make miniatures of things. But perhaps the best part of the market was the section for textiles. These were really marvellous: serapes (a sort of cloak) and skirts and bed-covers and carpets, all hand-woven and again all different. I found myself gaping cautiously at these stalls, cautiously because I hate bargaining. Well, it's no use hating bargaining in Mexico. It's positively offensive to have any such feeling, offensive to the man who's trying to sell you something. He doesn't care whether you buy or not, but he can't bear the idea that you won't even discuss the matter with him. It's the human contact that he wants and perhaps that's what markets have always been for, just as much as trading.

D. H. Lawrence once lived in Oaxaca for a few months and wrote a few chapters of his *Mornings in Mexico* about the place. He was in a good mood here for once, content to accept the Zapotecs for what they were, and not try and fit them in to some hysterical theory of his own. At one stall I was looking at a really superb rug showing swordfish in bright colours on a black background. Each of the sixteen swordfish had been done in a different arrangement of bright colours, and I was delighted again with this variety. The weaver had gone to a lot of extra trouble to make them all different, whereas in our mass-produced world I am sure he would have started repeating himself after half a dozen or so. Poring over the colours, to make absolutely sure he hadn't repeated, I fell into his trap. 'How much you give?' he said, and we were away. I tried to ignore him, but that was too rude. I suggested some wildly mingy sum, and he laughed and mentioned another as wildly exorbitant. I could see how the psychology of the thing worked. Ashamed at my first sum (after all he was dressed in rags, and seemed a nice fellow) I went up a bit. He came down a bit, but a vast number of pesos still separated us. This business went on for a while and we weren't getting anywhere. I thought I'd rather talk to him than bargain with him, so I suggested a tequila. Off we went to a cantina, where the tequila was poured out of a bottle shaped and painted like a monkey. The tequila didn't come out of the monkey's mouth but the middle of his head, where there was a cork. We had quite a lot of these tequilas and I learned the weaver's name was Luiz, he had made the swordfish rug himself, it took him two weeks, the colours were natural dyes he had manufactured himself from rocks and trees and cactus leaves, he lived at Tehuantepec, where the most beautiful women in Mexico are, he was 27, his father had been killed in the revolution (which revolution I couldn't make out), I should stay with him in Tehuantepec and he would introduce me to some of those beautiful women, because we were friends now, and: now was I sure I wouldn't buy that rug after all? And the price came down a bit. But I still wouldn't buy.

It was getting late in the afternoon, and I knew the radishes were soon to be on show in the square, and that's what I'd come to Oaxaca for, so I left Luiz with the rest of the tequila in the monkey-bottle and made my way in what was now gathering evening to the main square. Already I could hear the sound of a strange music, and when I came into the square there was a scene of the greatest charm. Playing on the Second Empire bandstand was a group of what I recognized as mariachi musicians. They are the equivalent of, say, a village band in Austria or a calypso group in Trinidad: not exactly folk musicians, but far from sophisticated either. Half of a mariachi band is strings, the other is brass, clarinets and so on. The mixture produces a sound of genteel raucousness, and there are flamboyant off-key songs sung in jerky snatches. The square was absolutely full now and the radish stalls were lined up in front of the big church where I'd been. I pushed into the crowd to get a closer look. The giant radishes were carved and knotted and spliced into the most extraordinary forms. Perhaps the majority were religious figures, usually arranged in groups appropriate to the season like Joseph and Mary by the manger or the wise men journeying towards Bethlehem; but others were political, and might show a meeting of politicians or trade unionists; and others again were sporting, showing, say, rather optimistically, Mexican footballers winning the World Cup. Others showed fish or animals or jet aircraft or trees or houses. It seems there's nothing you can't carve a radish into. A few were frankly obscene, but the Zapotecs don't divide the world up into categories as neatly as we do, and the function of all these radish sculptures was to be taken as offerings to decorate the Christmas cribs that every house has at this season.

I wandered happily round the square. A rather drunken photographer implored me to have my photograph taken seated on a donkey he had tethered to a tree. In one corner of the square bunuelos were being sold, sort of wafers like Indian poppadoms but soaked in treacle and just as nasty to eat as most Mexican food. They were worth buying though because you were served on a rough clay plate and the price of the bunuelos gave you the right to break the plate. There are few more satisfying feelings than smashing crockery. All round me happy Mexicans were chewing these horrible pieces of treacly cardboard and hurling their plates into the main road. Cars inched through the crowds with a marvellous crackling sound. As you strolled, the ground under you gave little crepitating sounds, as small fragments of plates broke into even smaller ones. It was like walking on biscuits. There was a fine feeling of the whole town being on the tiles. Some firecrackers went off; an Indian mother was feeding her baby under a street lamp; balloons filled with gas escaped from their strings and went up into the branches of the laurel trees, while small boys climbed on each others' shoulders to try and reach the strings; the band played; the noise of voices rose as if the square were a huge room at a party: and I thought this is all too much really, I must have a drink. I went down a side street away from the square and the band, and, whether by accident or design I'm not sure, found myself back at the cantina with Luiz the carpet-seller. He was well into another monkey-bottle of tequila and this time I was his guest. And the next time he was my guest, and so indeed seemed to be most of the other people in the cantina. But I felt I was in good company. I didn't mind what all this was costing or how late the time. I remember we had a lot of fun, but I can't pretend I remember every single thing about that night. What I do know is that I woke the next morning in my little white cell at the hotel, with rather less money in my pockets and with the swordfish rug folded neatly on the chair at the side of my bed.

PART TWO

EUROPE

7
Finland : The Russian Excursion
[July 1966]

LOOKING down at Finland under the wing of the plane, at the Baltic shining in the midnight sunlight and the hundreds of little offshore islands like jigsaw pieces, I sat and wondered how I was going to make sense of all these twelve countries in twelve weeks. I looked round the cabin at the other passengers, most of them Finns I could guess, but they were no help at all. The plane was more than half empty, and each person had taken a whole row of seats for himself. Now that wouldn't happen in Spain or Italy or Greece—no Greek could survive without conversation for three hours—but my journey was beginning far from the South, up here in the Nordic world where men are strong and separate and silent and unlikely to give anyone much help in making sense of them. Also this was high summer, when every Finn gets as far away from the cities as he can, hiding even from his fellow Finns in a country cottage in a pine forest by one of Finland's sixty thousand lakes where he can live for a month or two the simple life of his ancestors. Still, one would manage, and waiting for the lights of Helsinki I looked down at the green forests of Finland and the lakes etched in like on a map and then out at the tremendous Northern night sky, where the sun raged like a bonfire half round the horizon.

The first few summer mornings in any northern city like Helsinki are very strange. You wake with a guilty start to find sunshine pouring in, and you're furious that you've overslept and wasted a couple of hours of your precious week, and then you look at your

Finland: The Russian Excursion

watch and see that it's only four in the morning but broad day already. You get up anyway, and walk out. Helsinki is a marvellous walking city and I began each day by walking miles through the surprising and stylish streets. Later on I would sit and make those fruitless telephone calls to Finns who were away in their country cottages living the simple life, but first I'd start by exploring this city of the sea built on islands and promontories, where round every corner there's a gusty glimpse of big white liners or small quiet canals or the fish market with the gulls stooping to snatch herrings from the fishwives' baskets. Then as the city came to life this walking round the streets acquired an unwelcome spice, because the Finns are the worst drivers in the world. The sound of screaming tyres on the cobbles is the sound that will always bring Helsinki back to me. The Finns are great individualists, but that's not a policy that really works on the public highway.

During their famous war against the Russians in 1940, the Finnish soldiers, these individualists, were said to be the worst disciplined army in history, but they held up the Russians for many months because each Finn regarded the war as his own personal war against Russia. And today he's still waging war, only his weapon now is a car, and his enemy his neighbour.

Of course this individualist thing of the Finns also has some very attractive sides, and anyway I wasn't going to allow the screaming tyres to keep me from walking the streets especially as there was one very good reason to do so. This was the girls. I've never seen anything like them; they are one of the sights of Europe. For the first couple of days in Helsinki you get the impression that the population consists of young girls of about twenty with long blonde hair, of a quite melting freshness and prettiness, and with a most impressively independent air. After a while you do notice there are some other people in the streets, old ladies and men with briefcases and so on, but in fact there is a good reason for that first impression. For every two men in Helsinki there are three women, and a lot of the women are precisely girls of about twenty, born during the population explosion when soldiers came back after the war. And there's a reason for their air of independence too, because they've been brought up in one of the most fortunate societies in Europe: fortunate not because of wealth, because Finland isn't a rich country, but because here is somewhere where the sex war is really over, and has been for a long time. Finnish women were the first in Europe to get the vote, and they're equal with men before the law in every way. They do every kind of job. Even the Finnish representative of Interpol is a woman. Half the places in universities are filled by women and nearly a third of the doctors in Finland are women; but women also do heavy work, working in sawmills, or driving trucks, or sweeping the streets; and of course they have to bring up their families as well. In this sort of equality, equality of hard work and responsibility as well as just opportunity, I think Finnish women are very fortunate; and those pretty girls in the streets of Helsinki have good reason for their air of independence, because they're going to have the chance (unlike most women in Britain) to make their own lives.

Of course dodging the cars driven by Finnish individualists and doing a little gentle research on Finnish women was all very fine, but the week was passing and I still wasn't making much sense of the Finns. Then one night I had a stroke of luck. In a bar I met a cheerful man. Now the Finns are people of extremes. Either they're buried in bottomless introspection, with lips sealed tight, and staring sightlessly ahead, or else they have a few drinks and then they are cheerful to the point of lunacy. What was the cheerful man celebrating, I asked. 'I celebrate I am ruined,' he said, and he explained his firm had gone bust, he'd lost his job, and he was going to Leningrad to celebrate. Now this was very surprising to me: that any Finn should go to Leningrad to celebrate, should choose Russia, their traditional enemy whom they fear and hate, as the place to let their hair down. But it seems I'd stumbled on something. This is the great new Finnish version of the lost week-end: you take the train to Leningrad, eight hours and very cheap vodka once you've passed the border; sell a few shirts or ball-point pens on the black market in Leningrad and buy more vodka; roll around the streets under the shocked eyes of the Russians; then eight hours back to Helsinki drying out.

Now the Finns have very deep feelings about Russia, too deep and painful for them to talk about much, and I felt an expedition like this might be the great tongue-loosener. Alas, though, there was no question of my going to Leningrad with the cheerful man; he was going right away, and I had no Russian visa; but there was another trip, he said, that I could take without a visa, and that was the Sunday day-trip to Tallinn in Esthonia, across the Gulf of Finland and since the war, part of the Soviet Union. This, he went on, was a specially fascinating journey, because the Finns are closely related to the Esthonians; Finns and Esthonians are brothers, but in all the years since the war have been cut off from each other until these trips began recently. The Finns are related to nobody else on earth, except rather remotely to the Hungarians, and they feel this isolation badly, so they jumped at the chance of visiting their relatives across the water. As a matter of fact, said the cheerful man, cheerfully, there were a lot of illegal things going on. There was smuggling and espionage, and Esthonians were escaping to Finland, and the Finns were passing them over to Sweden without letting on to the Russians. In fact Finland would be badly placed if the Russians complained about these goings on, because Russia has only to huff and puff and the card-house of Finnish independence would tremble or even fall down, as it has done so often before. Over the centuries the Finns have fought forty-two wars with the Russians, and lost them all; and really the Finnish character has been formed by having the Russians as their neighbours. Plainly even a one day visit to Russia in Finnish company would be very interesting. Maybe this way I'd even begin to make sense of the Finns.

On the Russian ship at the quay by Helsinki fish market on Sunday morning I examined the other passengers with interest; but the Finns don't wear their hearts on their sleeves. In bright sun they sat there on the top deck, the men in dark suits and with their eternal hats, the women wearing plastic raincoats and carrying string bags full of corn flakes and coffee and lengths of sausage they were taking to Tallinn for relations or friends or just anybody they might meet; because Finns and Esthonians are brothers. As we steered through the islands and across the thirty odd miles of flat sea, a deep Finnish silence reigned on that deck. Those introspective faces with their sightless stares sent me below to the bar, where a handsome young Finnish couple were eating caviare sandwiches and drinking vodka through plastic straws. Their names were Kyosti and Maija, and they pressed me to the vodka, a very special sort called the Light of Esthonia and not to be missed, they said. True enough, and long before Tallinn we were fast friends. After a while, we went up to the deck and watched for Esthonia, and when Esthonia came in sight, well, it was just like Finland: low shores, pine trees, a spire and a few chimneys. The first sign of anything different was the welcome.

Everybody waved at us: sailors in fishing boats, men on the deck of a freighter, a boy on a barge—everybody waved frantically, as if we were the first visitors ever from the outside world. The next surprise was the quayside, and a crowd of three or four hundred at the barrier. Kyosti spoke to one of the crew and translated. 'He says they wait for every ship from Helsinki like this, since the service began three months ago. Of course they never know who will be on the ship.'

The Russian customs came on board and the crowd waited at the barrier. We signed declarations swearing that we were carrying no 'plants, fruits, seeds, or live animals or birds'. The customs men searched through those string bags full of corn flakes and German sausage, while the crowd at the barrier craned and peered to find faces along the ship's rail, and we in turn stared back, some of us more intently than others. Kyosti explained that a group of three middle-aged women at the rail were Esthonians returning to Tallinn after twenty years: they'd fled to Germany when the Russians came. They were searching the crowd too but they didn't seem to find anything—or anyone. Now we were closer and could see the family resemblance between the Esthonians and the Finns: brothers indeed, but one poorer than the other. We got ashore and pushed our way through people who searched our faces in turn. I saw an old lady and a middle-aged man from the boat embrace tearfully, but otherwise there didn't seem to be many meetings. Twenty years is a long time. We expected nothing of course and we walked on as tourists into the town, my friends stopping at every excuse to talk in their Finnish that is so like Esthonian: talking to a flower-seller, stopping in a shop for a chat and a foul lemonade, once being stopped by a young man who wanted to buy for useless Esthonian currency anything we had to sell: nylon shirts, American cigarettes, watches; but when we had nothing, he walked along with us and asked us about Finland and all the wide world he would probably never see. He was a polite young man, and he went away with a handshake and a warm smile. He was wearing ragged trousers and sandals tied with a piece of string.

We wandered through the tree-lined streets of the ancient town: Tallinn is eight hundred years old, a mediaeval city that hasn't changed. There were few cars in the streets, and the buildings hadn't been painted for decades: not since, indeed, the Russians came here at the same time as they came to Finland, at the beginning of the last war. In so many ways sad Tallinn today must be like what Helsinki was during that time before the war, indeed would be today if the Finns had been unlucky, or less diplomatic in their dealings with the Russians. We walked on past the old town hall and the theatre and the great mediaeval church and the castle and the statue of Lenin; and gradually, I noticed, my Finnish friends became silent, no longer speaking to passers by but instead smiling at them in a conspiratorial way, as if seeing themselves in a mirror image: this is what they might have been. Watching this as an outsider, I began at last now to make a little sense of the Finns. In Helsinki I had seen what they are today; now I was seeing how they might have been if they hadn't had the independence of those girls in the streets of Helsinki, or the cussed individualism of the soldiers who fought the Russians, each man waging his own private war. With all the geographical dice loaded against them, the Finns have survived and prospered; they've made a good life on the unlucky side of Europe.

8
Sweden: The Perils of Affluence
[August 1966]

I LIKE Sweden, and on the whole I was pleased to be in Stockholm again, that beautiful city, sitting on the hotel terrace watching the light glancing off the water in the busy harbour. Opposite, next to the island on which the Old Town stands, a big ocean liner was moored, its masts standing high above the eighteenth-century houses. Seaports are always exciting when the ships come right up into town, and I was happy to sit there on my third morning in Stockholm and watch the world go by. At the same time I was just a little uneasy, because in the last few hours I'd noticed a feeling coming over me that I knew I wasn't going to be able to shake off. This was a sensation I'd felt in Stockholm before, every time I'd been here, something like the first pricklings of a sore throat that tells you you're in for flu; only in this case it was a feeling of irritation and frustration, which I've discovered comes to many visitors to Stockholm after the first few honeymoon days of looking at the beautiful girls and the lovely buildings. It's a feeling of bafflement, of frustration as I say, and rejection—rejection by the city and its charming people. Why can't I get closer to them, the traveller thinks furiously, why is there this weird glass wall between the Swedes and myself? For a while you think that it's your fault, that there's something wrong with you that you can't get through to them. The first time you are in Sweden you have to live with this feeling for a few days, not knowing what to do about it, but I had been here before, and when I felt that first prickling of resentment at not being able to penetrate the glass wall, I knew that the fault (if that's the word) wasn't mine. I knew that the glass wall was really there, and that it cuts the Swedes off from each other as much as from foreigners.

This is the great Swedish malaise, the worm in the bud that makes Sweden a less than perfect place. Of course it should be no surprise to find that Sweden is less than perfect. The wonder is that it's as perfect as it is. As I sat on my terrace with the ships and the town in front of me, I read the paper. It was an English paper, but on one page there was a picture of a pretty smiling Swedish girl with a Come to Sweden sort of advertisement underneath, which read: 'Why is the pretty girl smiling? Because she lives in a country where everybody has a job and enough to eat, where crime is practically non-existent and there are no slums or ghettos, and there hasn't been a war for 150 years.' Well, that's right, and if there ever existed the conditions for The Good Society, where everybody has enough and is looked after properly, those conditions exist in Sweden today. This is probably the most prosperous and the most honest and fair country that's ever been, and yet one evening at a dinner party I was at in Stockholm a charming and well-dressed Swede of some importance in his country broke into the conversation by saying with a wail in his voice 'Oh, why are we so unhappy here in Sweden?' and he was right. There's a character in Strindberg who says 'Yes, it's true that life has given me all I asked, yet everything's turned out to be worthless to me. That is my curse,' and another Swede who has understood very well the curse in Swedish life is the film maker Ingmar Bergman. In his film *Wild Strawberries* one of the characters suffers from hallucinations in which he meets an inquisitor. 'What is my crime?' he asks, and the inquisitor answers 'Indifference, egotism, lack of feeling'. 'And what is my punishment?' 'The usual one,' the inquisitor replies, 'loneliness.' It's this coldness, this sense of isolation and loneliness, this impersonality in Swedish life that produces that baffled feeling the visitor has of being shut out by a glass wall.

The Swedes know about their malaise, of course, and of course they wish they didn't suffer from it. Under the placid and ordered surface of Swedish life, there is a lot of strain and unhappiness. It comes out in all sorts of ways. For instance, Sweden is famous as the country where the sexes are supposed to get on in a sensible way. The Swedes are not frightened of sex, nor are they anything like as promiscuous as malicious people make out. They have a proper idea of the worth of women, and women play a big role in Swedish life (one member of parliament in five, for instance, is a woman). Everything seems right then for a proper relationship between the sexes, for marriages that really are marriages, real partnerships of a kind that we in England don't have often enough: yet time and again in Sweden I've heard bitter accounts from men and women of lack of communication in marriage, of silent marriages where affection is buried too deep to find, where each partner is locked in the glass cell of his own ego.

This is the loneliness that the inquisitor in the Bergman film was talking about. Of course it happens everywhere, but in Sweden somehow more than most places. How strange it is to find, for example, that Swedish women, surely the most beautiful in the world, are often touchingly amazed when you tell them so, and they half don't believe you, because Swedish men never make this kind of remark, out of this same coldness we are talking about. The coldness comes into so many things. I was told the story of an American just moved into a Stockholm suburb, who rushed the child of neighbours he didn't know to hospital in his car in an emergency. The neighbours never came to thank him: instead they sent a note and a bunch of expensive flowers for his wife. The Swedish attitude towards children is strange too. Children are cared for with devotion, and every resource of the state is there to help them. From the point of view of education and health and welfare, Sweden is the perfect country to be a child in, yet the Swedes just don't have children. The most prosperous country in the world has very nearly the lowest birth-rate. It's as if the Swedes had lost their nerve, or despaired, and perhaps it's also that 'indifference, egotism, lack of feeling' that the Bergman character was talking about. Swedes don't like to be committed, partly by the way for a very good reason, because when they are committed, they take their responsibilities very seriously. If they do have children, they don't neglect them.

This unwillingness to be committed is very strong. In Kungsgatan, the sort of Piccadilly of Stockholm, I saw a small traffic accident. A motorcycle ridden by the leather-jacketed young Swedish equivalent of a rocker ran into a car, not very hard, but he was thrown off and lay in the road. The driver of the car had a look at him, and then went into a telephone kiosk and phoned for an ambulance. Then he waited with the boy for the ambulance to arrive. There were dozens of people around, but nobody came forward out of either curiosity or charity. I was puzzled by this indifference, but a Swedish friend explained to me that the matter was under control, there were established ways of handling such things and the ambulance was coming, there was nothing anyone could do and no necessity to get involved. He was being very reasonable, of course, but I thought altogether too reasonable: wasn't society getting too highly organized when you could make a doctrine out of 'I am *not* my brother's keeper'. I don't want to sound too carping, though. As I say, many Swedes find this coldness of theirs extremely distressing, but Swedes are rather rigid people and Sweden's a very rigid society, where it's not easy for someone to step outside the accepted way of behaving. For someone to step out of the crowd in that street would have been almost eccentric behaviour, and Sweden is a society where conformity is very important.

Swedish formality is famous, or notorious, though I must say I often find it rather charming. A Swedish dinner party is an experience; the elaborate protocol of one's arrival, greeting the hostess and the host and meeting the other guests, trying to remember their professions rather than their names, because until you know a man quite well you call him Mr. Company Director or Mr. Bank Manager rather than by his surname let alone his Christian name; then you sit at table and the strange ritual of *skalling* begins, where you lift your glass to each of the other guests in turn, and fix him with a beady stare while you both bottoms up; and the evening ends with what seems to be about half an hour spent thanking the hostess. By now one is a bit bored, but it's all harmless enough.

In the more serious affairs of life, I'm not sure that this passion for conformity is harmless. It comes into practically everything. Because of the passionate desire for everybody to agree with everybody else, Swedish politics has practically come to a standstill. The same party, the Social Democrats, have been in power for 33 years, and the present Prime Minister, Mr. Erlander, for twenty. Swedish politicians have some inducement to show off, because Parliament is televised, but they never do. Similarly unruffled are the relations between politicians and industry, and between industry and labour. Labour relations in Sweden would send the I'm All Right Jack type of British trades unionist into a dead faint from sheer disbelief.

Labour and Capital regard themselves as having a mutual responsibility to make the country prosper. 'Strikes are not a weapon that we use,' said a Swedish trades union leader. 'They are out of date.' Instead everything is done by mutual consent and nobody ruffles the waters. This is not just conformity, or rather the conformity stems from reasonableness. Swedes are the most reasonable people I know. Everything is done in the light of reason. Statistics are collected—they are also the most statistically-minded people I know—possibilities are weighed, and then the best decision is made for the good of the whole community. This is the key to Swedish prosperity and modernity. It stands to reason that if Labour and Capital regard themselves as members of the same family thrashing out a family problem, then they will arrive at a sensible solution more quickly than we can in this country with our cat-and-dog system.

To take a completely different example, civil defence: civil defence in Sweden is an eye-opener. Reason has been put to work, statistics assembled and decisions taken, and the decisions have been carried out. As a result Stockholm (which hasn't seen a shot fired in anger for 150 years) is the best defended city in the world. One afternoon I walked through a couple of the air shelters, vast Aladdin's Caves proof against any H-Bomb, used today as car parks and supermarkets. Two million people in Sweden can be accommodated underground, there's food and fuel for many months, half the nation's hydro-electric power and whole factories are down there. This preparedness for a presumably long chance is the most impressive example I saw of Swedish reasonableness. It's a reasonableness that ought to make for The Good Society, if we are to believe every reasonable man who's spoken since Voltaire and John Stuart Mill; but this hasn't happened, the Swedes haven't quite achieved The Good Society yet, and they know it. Why? Are they too materialistic, as is sometimes said? Not really. Money is valued in Sweden, but valued even more is what's done with the money. There are many rich people, of course, but it's quite common for them to regard their riches as held in trust for the community, to believe that it's their responsibility to use their money to do good. The case of Alfred Nobel, who used the money he made out of armaments to found a Peace Prize isn't unique. And taxes in Sweden are the highest in the world, the money going to create a welfare state that knocks ours into a cocked hat.

What is wrong, then? Too much conformity? A stifling of individuality? Perhaps; but there are contradictions here too. In this land of conformity, there is no censorship whatever of printed matter and the only scenes that are cut from films are scenes of violence. There is great tolerance of the misfit, the delinquent, the addict, the criminal: some Swedes would say far too much tolerance. What there isn't tolerance of, and here we may be coming near the point, is individuality, unusualness, excellence. In Sweden everybody is equal, and no one is allowed to be more equal than anyone else. An unattractive quality of many Swedes (which other Swedes will admit) is envy: the Royal Swedish Envy they call it. If a Swede talks about Ingmar Bergman, or Ingrid Bergman, or Greta Garbo or Erik Carlsson, the rally driver, or Dag Hammarskjöld—any Swede who's made his name in the world—it's very often, I'm sorry to say, in a denigrating way. It's no accident that all these famous folk are loners, who found their own way in the world, and no accident either that Swedish people are great joiners: everybody in Sweden belongs to a dozen clubs and associations and committees; and in this, I think, the Swedes betray themselves, because they are not natural joiners, and they are natural loners.

Sweden is a huge country and the Swede is a countryman. Today 85 per cent of Swedes live in the new prosperous cities, but at the beginning of the century only 25 per cent did so. A Swede really belongs in a huge, rather desolate underpopulated landscape where the next farm and his nearest neighbour is miles away. He lives a life of silence with his own thoughts. And he is still a solitary by nature, who perhaps doesn't make a very jolly marriage partner, but has huge reserves of the mind. By coming to the town, by engaging himself in the community, he has betrayed his nature, or rather his natural individuality, which will take a little time to assert itself in this new situation. When it does so, when the Swedes insist again on their separate individuality, we will hear a great deal of them. They already have the most efficient working society in the world. What they want now is to make that society work for them, and not the other way round. The Swedes are people of soul, and today they're waiting for their souls to catch up with them.

9
Germany : Berlin by Night
[August 1966]

I WON'T forget my first sight of Berlin on a strange Christmas Eve nearly twenty years ago now. Every time I go back, and I've just been back, I remember that evening, staring out of that aircraft and looking for the lights of the city. It was dark, and cloudy as well, and even after we fastened our seat-belts we didn't see anything at first. Then the Kurfürstendamm came through the cloud right below, just a straggle of lights with in those days hardly any neon and only a few cars, but still recognisably a street in a big city. The plane tilted to find the runway at Tempelhof, and suddenly all the lights disappeared. There was a row of street lamps along one straight road, actually the Bülowstrasse, and then nothing: blackness. I realized that this black spot was the centre of Berlin, the place where the bombs had been, and further over, where a few feeble lights showed beyond the blackness, was East Berlin. The Kurfürstendamm by comparison was a riot of light.

As soon as I got into the city on that Christmas Eve of 1950, I started to walk. I walked all night. I walked to the top of the Kurfürstendamm where the ruins of the Kaiser Wilhelm Church were (and still are); then I set out into the blackness. It's odd to reflect today, when West Berlin is as modern and prosperous as any other West German city, that in 1950 there was scarcely a single building intact in the three-quarters of a mile central Berlin between the Kurfürstendamm and the Potsdamerplatz. I walked on for an hour in and out of the network of well-repaired roads dividing city blocks almost bare of houses. In the Lutzowplatz, now a smart and very well-heeled looking square, there was nothing at all then, nothing that is except a Christmas tree in the middle of the square, lit by naked electric bulbs, a Christmas tree standing there on Christmas Eve in the middle of Berlin with no one at all to look at it for nearly a mile around except myself. I think that's the first time I really understood the meaning of war, and of Berlin as essentially a city of war, the city of Coriolanus. It's a city of war for one main reason: geography. Berlin stands between East and West, and I don't mean just in terms of today's politics. Berlin is the last frontier of Western Europe: to the West are the hills and rivers that have held back the enemies of Europe for twenty centuries, to the East are the great plains that stretch beyond Russia as far as the Pacific.

The tragedy of Europe in our time, of course, is that this division between East and West has persisted. Even in 1950, when the Berlin Wall wasn't thought of, the division was obvious enough in Berlin. I remember that I walked past the Christmas tree in the Lutzowplatz and across towards the Potsdamerstrasse, and picked my way through the gardens of ruined houses along a dirty canal until I came to the Potsdamerplatz itself. Today this is merely part of the Wall; then it was the meeting place of the British and Russian Sectors. The huge square, once a sort of Piccadilly Circus of Berlin, stood dark and empty in the freezing cold. The silence was broken only by the boots of the guards on the cobbles on the Soviet side, and once, in a brief moment of alarm, by the sound of a car on the Eastern side of the square accelerating away sharply with a squeal of tyres. I was younger in those days, and I think I got a thrill from that, and in a way correctly so, because those tyres could well have been squealing in earnest. Berlin then was a place where life was stranger than fiction, where a bump in the night meant business, as it sometimes does today. On that night sixteen years ago I walked across the Potsdamerplatz and into the Soviet Zone and for hours walked the empty streets there, wandering among the ruins of Unter den Linden and across the desert of the Karl Marx Platz to the untidy huddles of the Alexanderplatz, once the Oxford Street of Berlin, and then through the shambles of Prenzlauer until I came back to the West where I'd left it, at the Potsdamerplatz. I walked down the Potsdamerstrasse to the cafés clustered by the overhead railway. Those were rough days in Berlin, and the Spielcasino there, the neighbourhood gambling shop on the corner of the Bülowstrasse, was a gathering place for crooks of every kind. Smugglers between East and West used the place a lot, and currency deals were done there; but it was also a hangout for lonely people who wanted to talk, night people who had no reason to go home; and Berlin after the war was full of people like that, people whose families were dead or gone to live elsewhere.

Berlin seemed to me then the world capital of misery. Every night I used to go down to the Spielcasino and the other bars in the Potsdamerstrasse and pick up people to talk to, or rather to listen to their extraordinary stories of life in Berlin during the war and after. You could have conversations like this in East Berlin too, in the coffee shops and bars along the Friedrichstrasse, and there you noticed the same things: the confidence that all Berliners had (and have) that Berlin will one day again be the capital of Germany; the notion that so many Germans still have that they lost World War II by accident somehow; and the determination that they have not to make any more mistakes like that. These could be frightening ideas to listen to, but I find they come better from the Berliners than from some West Germans. The Berliners aren't without their share of Germanic self-pity, but they also have a most attractive style in irony and self-mockery. If they give you the creeps now and then, you do still feel they are the proper spokesmen for Germany.

I have been back to Berlin many times since that first strange Christmas visit and I don't think the place changes much. I don't think even the Wall has made all that difference. I'm not belittling the importance of the Wall. There is no man-made sight in the world to compare for shock value with one's first sight of this monstrosity, but far too much easy propaganda has been made over the Wall. This cashing in by the West on the suffering that the Wall has caused has now reached a real climax of nastiness, as I discovered the other day. The Wall has become a tourist attraction. Tourists visiting Germany are enjoined not to miss the chance of a personal peek at this symbol of Communist inhumanity, and guided tours to Berlin to see the Wall are arranged as part of programmes that include the Rhine castles and the Fasching beer festival in Munich. This is possible because any but West Berliners are permitted to cross the Wall into the Soviet Sector without hindrance, providing that they cross at certain points. The main one is near the Kochstrasse

Underground station, known to everybody as Checkpoint Charlie. Checkpoint Charlie is a sight for sore eyes. On the Soviet side it's ordinary enough except of course for the absolutely extraordinary fortifications, but on the West side of the barrier there is a strange little street of shops that sell souvenirs for the tourists to take home to Wisconsin or Wimbledon: souvenirs like cufflinks with the Brandenburg Gate emblazoned on them, or a glass model of the bear from which Berlin takes its name filled with egg-nog, or, almost unbelievably, a beer stein cast in the shape of a jackboot. There are postcards for sale showing the barbed wire of the wall, or the derelict buildings along the border area, or the graves of people who have been shot trying to cross the wall. They are very definitely not the sort of holiday postcards on which to write 'Wish you were here'. When you've bought your postcards you can visit a small museum full of horrific photographs of incidents at the Wall. All over the place are propaganda slogans about Freedom and Democracy—so insistent that you never want to hear those words again.

If you stand around in this strange little village of misery for half an hour or so, you'll probably see one of the tour buses. They're great double-decker affairs with glass sides so that the blue-haired ladies won't miss any nuance of the great melodrama being played out for their pleasure. They drive from the big hotels in West Berlin with a guide who tells them about the enormity of the Wall and the sufferings of the Berliners and makes little jokes about how he hopes they will get back safely from their adventurous journey to the other side. Then at Checkpoint Charlie they pass through the usual customs and currency inspection and the big bus crawls round the concrete obstructions carefully put there by the East Germans so that no one can rush the barrier. Then they're given a jaunt through East Berlin with a Communist guide pointing out the achievements of the regime. (Actually the only one of these guides I came across seemed modest and sensible.) Then I suppose they come back to their expensive hotels and gossip about the great adventure.

I don't know, it wasn't the way I wanted to see Berlin again. I thought instead that a night journey on my own would be more the thing, like the journey I made around the city that Christmas Eve sixteen years ago. This time I spent longer in the West and ended in the East. Berlin has always been famous for the eccentricity of its night life, and I thought I'd take a look at how this was going on today. All I could manage was a very modest sampling, because there must be more night life in Berlin than in any other city I know, except perhaps Tokyo. I'm told there are over six hundred *nachtlokale* in West Berlin, but I tried to pick out the odder ones. They are not as odd as they used to be. I couldn't find one of my old favourites, where instead of a dance floor there was a circus ring with a live horse tethered to the bar. If you felt like taking a ride, a couple of marks would secure you the horse for five minutes, but the main attraction was a bareback riding act performed by one of the bargirls. Then there used to be a strip-tease act off the Kurfürstendamm where the stripper threw the garments as she peeled them off to a baby elephant who caught them with his trunk. There are still strip-teases all over the place, and the strangest I saw this time was a girl dressed as a bride stripping on her wedding night before getting into a four-poster bed in the middle of the dance floor. More traditional is a place like the Resi, which has been going in Berlin since the Wicked Twenties. Today it's about as wicked as a Sunday School picnic. The floor show consists of what they call a water ballet, which is just jets of coloured water squirting in tune to schmaltzy music played by a gipsy band. What is supposed to be so wicked is the telephone on each table. There's a plan of the whole establishment on the back of the menu, and each table has a telephone number, so if you want to pick up a girl you ring her up and invite her for a dance. Unfortunately, whatever it may have been like in the Twenties, the Resi has become a family sort of place, so the girl nowadays is very likely to be out with her husband or her father, and you'll ring in vain. There's also a postal system between the tables through those pneumatic tubes that sometimes bring you your change in old-fashioned department stores, but I understand all messages go to a central pool before being delivered, and the naughty ones are weeded out.

Obviously, then, night life in the West was not going to drive me delirious, so I crossed over to the East, the usual laborious procedure with passports and so on via Checkpoint Charlie and the Wall instead of the old easy, spooky way across the Potsdamerplatz. What I found on the other side was tamer than before, and much nicer, and nicer certainly than the stripper with the elephant or the one on her wedding night. In spite of what you may have heard about the dullness of the place, there is a night life in East Berlin, and a very charming one too. There are a dozen or so dance places, where boys and girls go and married couples and families too. They are more like private parties than night clubs. If there's a floor show, it's a simple one, just a singer or two, perhaps a group; more likely there's just dancing and drinking and sitting around. Everyone dances with everyone else and there's a nice feeling of equality and anyone's as good as anyone else. It's fairly cheap and nobody tries to cheat or bully you into buying what you don't want to buy. You can't (as in the West) buy any of the girls, but much better, you can make friends with them. I found the whole atmosphere a nice change from West Berlin with its greedy passions, but Berlin is Berlin, and when the band packed up at four o'clock and I walked across the sleeping city to Checkpoint Charlie and bed, I couldn't say that Berlin was a town I'd like to live in. It's that line across the middle that spoils it, the inescapable Wall. When I got to Checkpoint Charlie, it was five o'clock and quite light, but there was nobody around except the few sleepy guards, and the morning air was fresh as the country. My papers were stamped, and I walked across the no man's land between the two worlds. In places the barbed wire had rusted and the concrete was splitting, showing a few blades of grass. Suddenly, from behind a gun emplacement, a couple of rabbits skipped out and ran across the road, and I felt for a second as if nature had at last taken over the suffering city and I was the only man on earth.

10
Poland : The Cool Generation
[July 1966]

I WONDER where else in the world would you be invited to a drinking party that began at ten in the morning? My host was a boy called Witold. He's a student in a technical college in Warsaw and he lives with his parents, and his two sisters, and his uncle and aunt in a *two-roomed* flat in one of the suburbs. The occasion for the party was that the uncle and aunt had taken the girls out for the day, and for a few rare hours until his parents got back from work, Witold and his friends had the little flat to themselves, to drink vodka and dance and play the fool. When I arrived at what I thought was the tactful hour of eleven in the morning, there were already a dozen or so young people rocking and rolling wildly to some vintage Elvis Presley discs. The vodka was going down rapidly and there was heavy petting in the bedroom. Hardly anybody in Poland today has a place of his own and an opportunity like this was precious.

Witold, my host at that party a few days ago, is about twenty-one, and his friends about the same. They look a little older: people in Eastern Europe always seem to look older than they are, but in fact in Poland today more than a third of the population is twenty-one or younger, and there's a special significance in being twenty-one in Poland this year. Witold was born in Warsaw in the early days of the Russian liberation which began on 17 January 1945, after the Soviet Army, in one of the most ruthless acts of history, had delayed their advance so that the Germans left in Warsaw had time to lay the city flat and crush the Polish resistance. In Poland, that day when the Russians came twenty-one years ago is the day that divides the past from the present. Anybody born after then has never known the old Poland, and Witold and his friends have grown to their full height without knowing life under any other system than Communism. What I went to Poland to find out was—are they different because of this? Are they less Polish then their fathers were? And remember that 'Polish' throughout modern history has meant a tremendous determination to be independent and free.

Well, at first sight Witold and the others seemed to be much like young people in England, different only perhaps in being less fortunate. To start with they are terribly poor. Students with state grants like Witold are considered to be the lucky ones, but after they've paid their board and lodging they've got about four pounds a month to spend. As a result they have to try and get jobs on the side; and indeed most people in Poland do a second job, if they can get one. Our party that day had to be over at half past three in the afternoon because Witold's father and mother came home at four for a bite and a rest before starting on their evening jobs. Witold went off to give an English lesson and I went off with his friends to a café, where they would spend the rest of the day, making a couple of cups of coffee last all afternoon and evening, just so as not to have to go home to their own flats and their teeming families. This overcrowding is the worst thing in Poland today. I went to a students' hostel and saw the rooms, each about the size of a large bathroom, where in term-time four students sleep and work. In Poland young couples meet, go courting, marry and get divorced without ever being alone for more than a few hours at a time. Yet the young Poles don't complain much. They try and make the best of things. The girls especially are quite heroic. At another party I made some feeble remark about what a mess we all looked (we'd been dancing, leaping about, and it was a hot evening) and then I caught a small hurt look on the face of one pretty girl and I realized that she thought I meant really a mess, and she didn't want to look a mess. She wanted, and deserved, the smart clothes she couldn't get. I saw some of the designs of the state fashion house, Moda Polska, and they were the opposite of thrilling. Tipped off by a visit I made to Poland a couple of years ago, this time I'd brought to friends some patterns my wife had collected from fashion magazines, and if I'd brought fairy gold I couldn't have given more pleasure. Out of their tiny students' allowances, these girls will practically starve themselves to save up for long white stockings or leather boots, and a Beatle disc fetches seven pounds on the black market.

This is because the Beatles are *Obcy*, a Polish word meaning foreign, and most things *Obcy* are thought good, especially where music is concerned. The jazz clubs of Poland are famous, and every night in the Stodola in Warsaw you can hear excellent imitations of Elvis and Cliff, the words sung in English by Polish boys who can't speak a word of English but have learned like parrots from listening to the original recordings. The Stodola wouldn't be thought great shakes by British teenagers. It's a homely place, rather like an old-time North Country dance hall, with an atmosphere of beer and sweat as thick as a Mersey fog. The other Warsaw dance places are similarly rather old world, just as their jazz heroes, Elvis and Cliff and so on, are on the whole our heroes of yesterday. Another dancing place is the Manikin Club in the main square of the old city of Warsaw, this one a copy of a Paris existentialist cellar of just after the war, with Picasso-like drawings and French obscenities scrawled on the walls. It's a bit absurd, but its *Obcy*, it's foreign, that's what matters. Not absolutely everything foreign fascinates, though. A lot of nonsense has been talked about Polish hunger today for Western ideas. There are indeed plenty of bookshops in Warsaw with foreign translations, but these are mostly of safe classics, and none of the students I talked to seemed especially upset at not being allowed to read, say, *Doctor Zhivago* or *Animal Farm*. You can buy foreign newspapers too, but the only person I ever saw seeking knowledge in this way was a boy reading the sports page of the *Daily Mirror* laboriously with the aid of a dictionary.

The young Poles long for Western luxuries like cars and clothes and the other bonuses of colour supplement living, but I don't think they really have any great envy of our conception of democracy or human rights or freedoms of speech. They seem to have agreed to cut their losses on that front. They just don't talk about politics any more; and it's not so much that they are afraid to, I think, as that they're not interested. They are materialists, and this is something new for the romantic Poles. This *is* a way in which they *are* different from their fathers, a way in which they *have* become less Polish. And the old Polish gift for satire and self-mockery seems to have grown less. People tell jokes against the government, but they are rather careful jokes. They have a satirical theatre in Warsaw, but the satire is domestic not political, all about mothers-in-law and lovers under the bed. I asked my student friends if they had a debating society in term-time and they thought this a curious idea. A couple of years ago a party of British students came to Poland, and my friends were not happy with them. 'They were strange,' one boy said to me, 'they had so many thoughts.'

Still, I don't want to sound too smart about this. If my friends in Warsaw are on the cautious side, they have plenty of reason to be. For a number of years after Stalin nobody was put in prison in Poland for his political opinions, but now people are going to prison again. I don't think any of the young people I met was a member of the Party or the Communist youth movement, but they were fairly careful not to be too obviously in opposition. Funny things happen. To take an absurd but powerful example—the *Playboy* case. Two or three years ago *Playboy*, the American girlie magazine, brought out an issue on Girls Behind the Iron Curtain. One picture showed a very pretty Polish girl in a provocative pose, but (unlike some of the Russian beauties) with all her clothes on. When the magazine came to the notice of the authorities in Warsaw they sent for this girl and put her through a lengthy grilling at police headquarters. She wasn't punished, just given a lesson. I made an appointment to see this lively girl but she never turned up. Several other people wouldn't see me either. As my hotel room was bugged, my telephone tapped and my mail steamed open, I wasn't surprised. On the whole though most people didn't mind meeting me, and I made a number of expeditions with my friend Witold, who gave that ten-in-the-morning party.

As a sort of object lesson in the class structure of the classless society, he took me one evening to Targowa, a long street on the East side of the Vistula, away from the fashionable centre of Warsaw, where we had a look at the underside of Polish life. In the long summer dusk the lurching carts and ragged beggar women and stumbling drunks were like a scene out of Gogol. The great thing was the drinking. Drinking in Poland is almost compulsory and drunkenness is regarded as an heroic failing. A bottle of 95 proof vodka costs less than ten shillings, and it's considered bad form to refuse to lend a man the money for a few drinks. The drinkers start young, and very sad are the *hooligani*, the Polish equivalents of our teddy boys. I say teddy boys, the teddy boys of a few years ago, because everything in Poland is like that, a few years out of date. Walking along Targowa street with Witold, we were approached by a very scruffy young man carrying an ordinary brick. He spoke to Witold and Witold translated: 'He says would you like to buy his brick?' Before I could say of course not, Witold said 'I would if I were you. Give him twenty zlotys, please.' I handed over this money (about five shillings) and the scruffy young man duly handed me the brick, smiled and walked away. 'If you hadn't paid,' said Witold, 'you would have got the brick anyway. In your face.'

That seems awful, but worse than the violence, I think, is a sort of moral breakdown in Polish life. Poland is the chosen land of the racket and the fast deal. There is a currency racket, a fuel racket, a housing racket. There are plenty of regulations against these rackets, but regulations in Poland are regarded just as obstacles to be overcome. No moral blame attaches to corruption, even in high places. A meat scandal involving five million pounds a year went on for years, until the conspirators over-reached themselves and murdered an official of the Ministry of Commerce during office hours in the lift of the Ministry building. Some of the rackets have a real beauty of invention about them. A syndicate of young men bribed officials at the state bus factory to give them private delivery of one of the buses, which they then ran for a year on the most profitable route in Warsaw, putting the fares in their own pockets. The worst of the rackets, a few years ago, was a racket in corpses, or rather in the clothes that the corpses were dressed in. In Poland you are buried in your best clothes and a good suit fetches a high price on the black market, so a racket developed in digging up corpses and undressing them.

I'm afraid I'm making Poland sound a horrible place, which it isn't quite. I was lucky perhaps in choosing to spend my week almost entirely with young people. The young Poles are gay and friendly and good-looking, and if they are a little tame, well, perhaps they have reason to be. They say: what else could they be? With Russia on one border, and the Germans on the other, what can they do but sit still and be good. This is how they've always been placed, but one seems to remember that their fathers didn't knuckle down so easily. Are they then, these young Poles, who were born and have lived all their lives under Communism, different from their fathers? I think they are. They have a word for themselves and their new attitude: *Zimny*, which means something like 'cold', in the sense of indifferent or passive: 'cool' is perhaps the best contemporary translation. They are the Cool Generation. What can't be changed, they have decided they won't try and change. What they can't fight, they will accept. They don't want fine phrases like freedom and human rights. They want sports cars and holidays in Spain and fashionable clothes. You could say they have given up, but they would say they are simply facing facts, facts that we in the West have never had to face. Some people have more difficult lives than others, and though I spent my time in Warsaw in the company of people half my own age, I can't say that I ever felt anything like twice as old—let alone twice as wise—as my Polish friends.

11

Germany: Taking the Waters, Playing the Tables
[August 1966]

I WAS lugging my bags out of the station when I saw the little old man. He had a long white beard, and he was sitting on the box of a four-wheel open carriage behind a horse that looked almost as old as himself, and the carriage looked older than either of them. The little old man climbed down from his perch and helped me with my bags and I spread myself on the hot leather seat and we trotted off into the town in fine nineteenth-century fashion. It was all a little corny, but the right way, I felt, to make my entrance into Baden-Baden, that prince of spas, the place where Queen Victoria took the waters and Dostoevsky lost his shirt at the Casino. In the last century everybody was at Baden-Baden: Kaiser Wilhelm I and Napoleon III put their heads together here; Turgenev held court among the Russian exiles and Edward VII played tennis and spruced up the race-course; and indeed by the look of the streets as we trotted along the whole lot of them might still have been here. The houses looked like cuckoo clocks with façades cut by fretwork and the cobbled alleys were coy illustrations to Hansel and Gretel. On the pavements were girls in embroidered skirts and in the distance there was a band playing Lehar and Strauss.

I sat there in the sunshine behind my driver, my aged retainer as I was beginning to think of him, and the only thing that spoiled the mirage as we trotted along was the screech of tyres and the exhaust fumes as the aggressive German drivers tried to elbow our poor old nag off the road. We took to the side streets, driving under shady trees between peeling villas, and my feeling of being transported in some sort of time machine to the days of Queen Victoria and Dostoevsky and the rest of them increased when I saw that the street lamps were all lit by gas, and increased still further when I noticed the extreme age and decrepitude of most of the people we passed. If I had been transported in a time machine, they plainly had been here all the time. We got to my hotel and the hall was full of grandfather clocks and the proprietor was a kindly shrivelled old lady older than Methusaleh. She led me to my room, and left me there as bewildered as a character in a fairy tale who doesn't know the story. I lay on my bed and gazed at a terrible painting of a stag at bay, and then I fell asleep, because last night had been a hard day's night in the *nachtlokale* of Berlin, and today had been a long day's journey to Baden-Baden.

Early next morning I set out to explore. I always hate the first few hours in a new town, the feeling that you don't know where anything is or where you are. The first thing I have to do is get a map and establish my bearing, but in Baden-Baden your bearings aren't hard to find, because this is a tiny place. The dimensions of a spa are really decided by the distance an invalid can be expected to walk, and this makes for a very cosy size. Baden-Baden is like a toy town, and very neatly arranged in this toy town are just four different kinds of buildings: hotels galore, a town of expensive hotels rather than private houses; then the various establishments for taking the waters, taking the cure; then (I was looking forward to this) the Casino; and finally the shops, some of the poshest shops in Europe, for the people who can afford the money to stay in the hotels and take the waters and who haven't lost it yet at the Casino. First, the hotels, and there's one of the great hotels of the world in Baden-Baden. It's called the Brenner Park, and it's an odd place. I wandered in there for a coffee, and was asked for my room number. When I said I didn't have one, I was asked to leave. This is one of those very rare hotels—I only know of one other in Monte Carlo—where you are not welcome if you're not staying there. As I was being propelled through the swing doors, I caught a glimpse of a late breakfast guest weighing himself on the scales at the entrance to the dining-room, I don't know whether to see if he'd gained any weight during the night, or to check how much he could eat for breakfast before going out to sweat it off in the steam bath at the spa. Outside I could see one of the reasons for my unfriendly reception; a ring of very nasty barbed wire running round the parapet of the first floor; and I remembered that a couple of years ago a guest at the Park Hotel had been relieved of five hundred thousand dollars' worth of jewellery.

I wandered on round the little town, past the house where Turgenev lived and past the Russian church where perhaps he went, with its bright blue onion dome where once a month a Russian Orthodox priest still conducts a service for a tiny congregation of the faithful. The church is nearly a hundred years old, and when I went inside I was back in the time machine again, with the morning sun creeping through the small high windows and a little old woman in a black shawl mumbling prayers near the altar. I wandered on past the Anglican Church nearby which is Norman in style and could easily be in a Suffolk village; past the house of the Mexican Consul, the only Consul in Baden-Baden and surely a man with time on his hands; and on into the residential district where every second house seems to have a doctor's nameplate on the gate. There are about a hundred doctors in this town, and the only thing there is more of is chemist shops. They're in every street, and inside with their mysterious wooden cabinets and huge bottles of coloured fluids they've got all that air of alchemy which continental chemists seem to have. Here, you feel, is a place where miracles might be done—or spells cast. The chemists are here, of course, like the doctors, because Baden-Baden is a spa with thermal waters that you bathe in to cure you of various things, like rheumatism and arthritis and liver trouble and what the prospectus of the spa engagingly calls 'professional diseases, injuries of civilization, and managerial ailments'.

Managerial ailments seemed to be what was wrong with a lot of the people I found making their way towards the bath-house, managerial ailments like eating too much to judge from the pasty faces. The bath-house itself was rather a let-down, no marble columns and cracked plaster sprouting weeds and moss, but all new concrete and shining chromium and glass. In the reception hall a severe young lady in a starched white coat was waiting for me: my guide. The whole bath operation was on several floors, and we began our tour on the roof, where there was a swimming pool of warm thermal water in which various sufferers from managerial ailments were wallowing or floating, their tummies sticking like bowler hats above the surface of the water. We passed on to the floor below where various other victims of civilization were having individual baths: oxygen baths for bad nerves, carbonic acid baths for weak hearts, steam baths for getting the weight down. Through each bathroom we caught a glimpse of a red face and hairy shoulders above the white porcelain, while at the head of the bath where the taps usually are stood a cold-eyed technician twiddling knobs and scanning dials. We got a glimpse of a mud bath where some poor fellow lay buried in a sack of volcanic lava. He gave me what I interpreted as a pleading glance as we went by, but I had no time for thoughts of rescue, because my own turn was coming. I'd elected to try what's known as the 'Kneippkur', a mixture of a health cure and an obstacle race aimed at toning up flabby citizens like myself. The young lady in the starched white coat made herself scarce and I stripped off and went into the large tiled room where the punishment was to be delivered. The room was divided into compartments or stalls and supervised by a couple of strapping attendants in bathing costumes, as muscular as lifeguards. I walked over to the first of the stalls and at once a jet of icy water hit me in the stomach. One of the lifeguards was using a hose on me, and after a few moments he switched the nozzle and the icy cold was replaced by boiling hot. Not a whimper passed my lips, and he rang the changes for a couple of minutes; then he motioned me into the next compartment where there was nothing but a pair of very large wooden boots filled with water. I was made to stand in these while the water slowly heated up until it reached unbearable point. I passed on to the next compartment where there was a tank full of water with two arm holes in the top. The thing had a nasty mediaeval look. I put my arms in the holes and the water began to heat up just like the wooden boots. The next stage was to sit in a tub while this same heating up process was repeated once again. Now I know what a boiled egg feels like. This tub was called a 'sitzbad', and the next stage was the 'sitzdousche'. I had to sit down on what looked like a lavatory seat, but instead of a lavatory pan underneath there was something like a garden sprinkler, sprinkling upwards, sprinkling my bottom from below: rather pleasant. I was getting near the end of the course, but the last obstacle was the most curious, where I was made to walk in a ring waist-high in water with some small pebbles underfoot. This, explained my instructor, if I understood him right, was to improve my circulation and 'restore my contact with nature'.

After all this I had a bit of a thirst, so I put on my clothes and set out for the Trinkhalle. This is a large hall near the bath-house where you can see some of the richest people in the world paying large sums of money to drink glasses of hot water. These captains of German industry and their hefty wives promenade to and fro, steaming glass in hand, and sip delicately at exactly the same sort of water they've just been bathing in. The water is about the same temperature as Japanese sake, but there's no pretending it's not water. There are several varieties, and the most any of them taste of is slightly salt or a sort of sodium bicarbonate taste: the stuff you used to give children who'd eaten too much. I drank a little of this for old times' sake, and a little more of a variety I was told was radioactive, hoping that later on I would glow in the dark like the face of a watch; but there really wasn't much to be got out of this water drinking, and I made my way towards a late lunch in the Casino restaurant. The Casino is the great ornament of Baden-Baden. It's a lovely building, tall white columns overlooking flowered lawns and a small rushing stream outside, and inside it's exactly what a Casino ought to be: elaborate chandeliers and damask-covered walls and Renaissance murals on the ceiling. In the restaurant, though, there was a real stench of rich food and that odd claustrophobic atmosphere that you find wherever Germans are gathered to do what they like best, which is to eat. All around me those sufferers from managerial ailments were undoing the good morning's work they had put in at the baths.

I went on into the Casino. Play was already well under way, and as usual the heady atmosphere caught one up at once. Surely a Casino is one of the handsomest places there is: the dark green tables with their yellow numbers, the shine of the low table lamps and the dramatic shadows they cast, the red flash of the numbers on the roulette wheel and the glint of silver on the spokes as they spin. And that's not to mention the excitement: the sense of being a serious place that a Casino always has, but a seriousness mixed with melodrama and hysteria and with greed, the dominant emotion in gambling. Of course greed isn't a very nice emotion, and that's why I was interested and attracted this afternoon by a young man at the first table I stopped by. They were playing roulette, and he was betting very high, but with a splendid casualness, as though he could afford to throw money away, although he didn't look as if he could. The others were all scribbling away on their pads, manipulating complicated systems, but the young man disdained these vain calculations, he used no pencil and paper or diagrams and he placed his bets only at the very last moment, just before the croupier called a halt and the ball rattled into its fatal slot. I watched him for half an hour, while he made perhaps ten thousand marks, or a thousand pounds; then I thought why not ride on his luck in my own small way, and I began to bet myself, five marks each time on the same numbers that he was putting a hundred marks on. I placed my chips on top of his and at once a curious thing happened. He began to lose, and I lost with him, of course. Half an hour passed, and I'd lost all I was prepared to: about ten pounds. In that time the young man had lost perhaps five hundred pounds. We walked away from the table together and I spoke to him for the first time: 'I thought you were going to bring me luck,' I said. He replied, in English: 'No, *you* were bringing me luck, when you were watching me. Then you made the big mistake. You began to play, and so we both lost.' He smiled. 'I will allow you to buy me a drink,' he said. We walked over to the bar, and I noticed on the clock that I had been exactly twenty-four hours in Baden-Baden.

12
Switzerland: Where the Money Is
[September 1966]

I ENTERED Switzerland at Zurich, where the gnomes are, and that was maybe a mistake. It was to see the gnomes and enquire about their activities that I'd come, but Zurich is a sombre place. It shouldn't be, with all its trees and parks and that lovely green mountain behind and the glittering lake in front, and perhaps it's the Zurichers I've never really got on terms with. They are good folk, of course, but they look so strange, with those folds of cream-cake-induced fat making them seem as if they had no necks, and they talk so oddly in their guttural Sweitzer-Deutsch, using diminutives all the time so that the bits you can understand sound like baby-talk. They use the itzy-bitzy 'li' after every second noun, even referring to the Alps as 'Usere Bärgli'—'our little mountains'. Still it was the gnomes of Zurich and their money I'd come to find out about, because this is the town with the proverb: 'God rules in heaven, but on earth money is master.' The man who told me this had another little saying, this time a German one: 'Money alone cannot bring you happiness, unless you have an account in a Swiss bank.' Needless to say, he had one: indeed he was the manager of a bank. I went to call on him there, in a vast, impressive, rather prison-like building in the Bahnhofstrasse. The severe look of the grey four-storey building was mitigated a little by the window-boxes of bright geraniums and by an eager little crowd on the pavement. Imagining, indeed rather hoping for, news of some sensational reverse on the world's exchanges, I peered over their shoulders and found they were staring at the permanent exhibition in the bank's show window, a little pile of gold bars on a velvet mat. Further along there was a board showing the latest stock prices on Wall Street: the prices are brought up to date every hour, and Zurichers watch them as keenly as racegoers watch the tote. That's the thing about money in Switzerland: everybody thinks about it. We think we think a lot about money, but what we're really thinking about is what we can use it for. The Swiss are not so much interested in possessions: they're interested in the money itself. Children in Switzerland are taught to save money before they know what money is, and Swiss toyshops are full of little Matterhorns and bears and Mickey Mouses with slits in: piggy-banks for Swiss children to learn the lesson of thrift. The average Swiss saves four times as much as we do; and in proportion to the population there's three times as much gold in Swiss banks as there is in Fort Knox. These were the sort of figures that I heard from the manager of that formidable bank when I got inside. This was one of the five Big Banks as they're called. There are over four hundred banks in Switzerland, but these five do about half the business, and are among the most powerful banks in the world. Indeed in Switzerland they are, for most purposes, rather more powerful than the state itself.

When I had negotiated the very distinguished-looking doorman with his grey frock coat, chatted up a pretty receptionist and a couple of over-well-dressed men in blue suits and gone up in an elevator that played soothing music, I found myself in a sober office with the manager, and he explained why Swiss banks are so powerful. It's partly because Switzerland isn't really a state, a country in the sense that other Western European countries are. To start with it's a Federation of twenty-five cantons with three languages between them, two main religions, and a thousand reasons real and imagined for distrusting each other. The duties of the central government are practically confined to defence, building roads, and foreign relations. The Swiss are intensely private people: they keep themselves to themselves, even among themselves. They're also distrustful of neighbouring countries, yet they have had to look for some function to play in Europe, and this history has found for them. For a long time nothing was easy for the Swiss. They had few advantages. Only seven per cent of beautiful Switzerland can be farmed, and the country has no minerals at all, so for hundreds of years the Swiss were forced to earn their living as soldiers, hiring themselves out as mercenaries to the highest bidder, and the Sweitzers (as they were called) were famous for hundreds of years for their courage and craftiness. Then came the persecution of the Protestants in France, and later the French Revolution, and these two events were the making of Switzerland. Switzerland was poor, France was rich, and the persecuted of France had to find somewhere to hide away their money. Thus were the Swiss banks created, and ever since the French Revolution Switzerland has profited from every upheaval in Europe, and more recently, elsewhere in the world, because Switzerland is secure. In a topsy-turvy world, said my friend the Zurich bank manager, if Switzerland did not exist, someone would have to invent us. As a result, this country with nothing has the fourth highest standard of living in the world, and a lot of enemies. After talking to dozens of people in Zurich, Berne and Geneva, I'm convinced that most unkind feelings towards Switzerland aren't justified, and particularly the attitude that we've had quite a lot in Britain this year and last, the self-pitying attitude that all our troubles are due somehow to the gnomes of Zurich casting a gnomish spell on our finances. Indeed the truth seems to be that if it wasn't for the Swiss banks and the Swiss attitude towards money we should be even more in the cart than we are.

Money is what keeps Switzerland alive, and what the Swiss have is a respect for money. This isn't as obvious as it sounds. As we sat there drinking hot chocolate in the sombre office above the Bahnhofstrasse, my bank manager friend made a remark which would sound like a joke spoken by a British banker, but he didn't smile at all. 'The banker, you see,' he said, 'he is like a lawyer, or a doctor, or maybe the best comparison is a priest. Yes, banking is a priestly calling, and perhaps that is why we are misunderstood by many. People speak of the secrecy of the Swiss banks. We keep our secrets in Zurich, yes, but only as a priest keeps the sanctity of the confessional.' Well, he was describing quite honestly the motives behind the famous secrecy of Swiss banks. That secrecy is stronger even than he said in fact. Not only *should* a Swiss banker not reveal anything about his clients, he is in fact *forbidden* to do so by a Swiss government law. If the Swiss authorities want to find out how much money either a Swiss or a foreigner has in his Swiss bank account, they haven't a chance; still less has a foreign government, however powerful. Swiss banks are audited by an over-riding National Bank, but the National Bank doesn't tell the government anything: if anything is wrong, it's a private matter between the National Bank and the bank concerned. Indeed there are a large number of Private Banks, as they're called, anyone can start a bank in Switzerland, and they don't have to publish any accounts at all. I'm sure you can see the advantages of all this—supposing you're a South American dictator on the make, or simply a film star trying to get out of paying so much tax in Britain or America. One difficulty is that you had better *be* a South American dictator or a film star, or they won't be very excited to hear from you. You have to be big stuff. If you're thinking of getting away from Mr. Wilson's austerities by settling in Switzerland and starting a little business, well, you won't get much encouragement from the Swiss. Too many people have tried to do that already. Even the tax evasion side of things is beginning to worry the Swiss, though so much money is involved for them that I expect they will allow themselves to go on being worried for a little longer. As my Zuricher bank manager said over the cooling chocolate, 'Of course we have to presume a large portion of our foreign customers are here for tax evasions,' and he shrugged his shoulders. When I asked him if he could help me evade my tax, he smiled sadly and said 'No, no, we do not deal with insubstantial people', so I swallowed my pride and made my way to Berne and Geneva a little wiser about the mysteries of Swiss banking.

But I was still intrigued by a system that, little benefit as it could be to me, had undoubtedly feathered some very comfortable nests. The secrecy of Swiss banks was no doubt admirable, and the banker as holy as a priest and all that, but surely there were spectacular opportunities here for every sort of skullduggery. The place to find out more about this would be one of the Private Banks, and Geneva is the place for these. They're in the old town in the streets that climb above the lake on the left bank of the Rhône. I crossed the bridge next to the splendid fountain that shoots three hundred feet in the air to fall like mist across the sugar-icing image of Mont Blanc etched against the dazzling blue sky and climbed up into the old town to find a staid building in the rue Diday. Luckily I knew the number because outside there was as little to identify the building as a London club. True, there were bars on the windows, but then this was Switzerland where everyone locks himself up as if under siege. The porter might have been a butler, and the girl with grey-green eyes in the black sweater the daughter of the house. There was no vulgar elevator here, and I was shown through the period furniture past the oil paintings of, I presumed, old captains of banking and up the stairs to a corridor with heavy doors opening off it. My host was waiting for me in a small reception room and we never went into his office at all. He had been prepared by a friend for my visit, or I should never have got into the house, let alone been allowed to ask questions about the shady side of Swiss banking. Yes, it was banks like this that handled the hot money that comes to Switzerland, he said, though never actually his own bank. They had turned down Trujillo of the Dominican Republic some years ago, they would always turn down any rascal like that. But—other bankers did take such money, and why should they not? He repeated the credo of the Swiss banker, a nice Latin phrase which says: 'Pecunia non olet'—'Money has no smell'. 'After all, you see,' he said, rather turning on his tracks I thought, 'people like Batista of Cuba, Peron in the Argentine, King Feisal in Iraq, certainly when they were in power they sent money here, to use in case one day they are not in power, but when they send the money they are the government of their country, the money belongs to them, like the money your Queen Elizabeth receives from the State.' I can't say I thought this was a very good parallel, but I asked to hear more about the dictators. 'Well,' my informant said, 'Batista was a disappointment to us. He took his money away and put it in the United States, in Miami. Very foolish. The Americans didn't want him to make trouble, so they froze his money in the bank. In Switzerland, that would be impossible, impossible for the government to discover even if he had any money in our bank.' I asked next about Communist money in Switzerland. He said he was sure there was some, used for paying their agents and also for investing in American industry. 'That way you make the other side work for you,' he said with a smile, but pointed out that there wasn't much of this going on. I asked if he thought there was any Russian investment in American armaments firms making weapons to use in Vietnam and possibly China. 'Don't ask me,' he said. I asked about the thorny old question of German-Jewish money sent to Switzerland before the war, and after the war claimed by Israel. He said this was much exaggerated, the Israelis had got some of the money, but I must remember that a Swiss bank never, repeat never, disclosed the names of its clients, dead or alive, or the amounts they had deposited. 'And remember,' he added, 'in Switzerland after twenty years money deposited in the bank and not claimed becomes the property of the bank, so that matter you speak of is now of course closed.' I remarked that this sounded pretty ruthless. 'No, we are not ruthless,' he said, and looked round the elegant reception room. 'We provide a service,' he said. 'Look at this house. Everything is for our clients. The service is personal. We do not use machines. Here you receive your bank statement written out with pen and ink. It comes to you in a plain envelope. We assist you in every way. Of course we charge you money for our services, but we make money for you. We do business as pleasantly as we can, but we do business, Switzerland is not a country, it is a business.'

13
Greece : The Real Greece
[September 1966]

WAS it all a mistake? I looked at the tourists in the pavement cafés and wondered if it was a mistake to have come back to Greece after so many years, back to the Greece one remembered so fondly. When I first went to Greece just after the war, Athens was a ramshackle Balkan capital with collapsing houses and holes in the streets, and there wasn't a single tourist in the whole country: it was a funny time to remember fondly, a time of civil war and poverty and not quite enough to eat. I had plenty to eat, being a pampered member of a British mission, but nearly all my time was spent with Greek people, usually poor people, and I learned to recognize in them a gaiety, a style, a verve, and a gift for happiness among all their troubles that over the years I came to think of as essentially Greek, to value enormously and to be afraid that they might have lost.

To a horrible degree the world these days is becoming all the same place, and on this trip through Europe I've been depressed again and again to see how everybody everywhere is getting to wear the same clothes, read the same sort of magazines, watch the same telly programmes, dance to the same tunes. With quite deliberate cowardice I'd kept away from Greece since 1950, not wanting to find that the Greeks too were going this way; and now driving into Athens from the airport in the same warm evening I felt how right I'd been, what a mistake it was to come back to these streets full of the same cars you see in other cities, with neons everywhere advertising the same airlines or drinks or films, the girls on the pavements wearing the same mini-skirts and the men carrying the same awful transistors, and the loudspeakers as we passed the Zappeion (the big park in the centre of Athens) blaring out the Beatles instead of the harsh, anguished strains of the Greek Bazouki.

In short I had got myself into a real old sentimental state of mind and everything for the next couple of days contributed to this. I used to live in the old Turkish quarter of Athens, the Plaka, and I went there this first evening to dine. I wandered through the little winding streets just under the Acropolis, and the streets were much the same as they always were but full now of strutting German tourists in leather shorts and awful young Englishmen with beards and their girls with dirty long hair, and my little feelings of resentment got worse and worse. Without actually saying to myself that this was *my* Athens they were mucking up, that's just about what I was foolishly feeling. I passed a house where once I'd spent many happy hours with the family of a Greek painter I knew, but the painter is famous now and lives in Paris, and the house has been sold and turned into a restaurant, and there I ate my dinner, among strangers in the great long room on the first floor where once I'd sat with friends. Athens by daylight the next day wasn't a bit better, with shiny office buildings in the place of the old Balkan untidiness, and those holes in the road all mended, and again everywhere the tourists, the young ones lugging their knapsacks and poring over their maps, the older ones queuing to post their postcards or gazing like goldfish out of the windows of their sightseeing buses.

Obviously in this vile mood of misanthropy the sooner I got out of Athens the better. Greece is a sizeable country, and there must be places where these people didn't go. I thought of the Aegean islands where I used to wander, but all islands have one great disadvantage: once you're there, you can't necessarily get off just because you want to, supposing you didn't find anything you liked. Still there was one island I had to pay my respects to, the place where I'd lived for two years whenever I could get away from my job in Athens, the island of Hydra in the Saronic Gulf only four hours from Athens. I had heard grisly reports in London of what had happened to Hydra; that films had been made there (always a fatal thing to happen to any pleasant place), and that the island was populated now by bearded poets and unappreciated painters and their hangers-on. I could understand why these awful people chose Hydra, because it *is* the island of islands, a dramatic narrow spine of rock five hundred miles long with nearly all the population clustered round a tiny perfect harbour from which a pretty painted town rises in a steep semi-circle like an amphitheatre. The Hydra people sit on their doorsteps and watch what's going on in the harbour below like spectators at a play.

Every day in Greece in summer is a perfect day, and I felt much less grumpy as the ship slid over the turquoise sea between dim purple island shapes under an utterly blue sky, and Athens became just a smoky smudge on the horizon. In general I'm in favour of travelling first class, because when you're first you can always move down, but when you're third it's a bit harder to move up, if that's where the interesting company happens to be. On Greek island boats in summer though, the first class is always full of tourists, and so I'd booked myself into the generous shambles of the steerage where there are no seats and the passengers sit or lie on the deck surrounded by all their possessions, which aren't just baggage but include vegetables and firewood and chickens and on this journey even a couple of goats. There are two Greek attitudes to the event of travelling: one is that it's not an event at all, and the passengers take no notice of their surroundings but simply continue the non-stop highly intense conversation that occupies most of the waking hours of every Greek; and the other attitude to travelling is that every journey is your last one. On a bus, on a train, on a streetcar, these people can always be found: usually fathomlessly old ladies with faces like walnut shells crouched in the cowering position of a child about to be born, like these two old crones lying with their faces of doom on the throbbing deck of the steamer to Hydra. Next to them a nanny goat worried at a piece of sacking, and an Orthodox priest sat on a bench with his black stove-pipe hat at an angle and a tape recorder on his knee. The tape was playing a Byzantine chant in contrast to the raucous 'Never on Sunday' sort of tunes coming out of the loudspeaker. All public places in Greece—a village street, a café, the deck of a ship—are filled with this sound of badly recorded and crudely amplified music to which nobody listens but which no one could bear to be without.

And so with a noise of pandemonium we sailed across the calm shining sea to Hydra. I strained in the din with my poor Greek to try and catch something of what people were saying, and with typical Greek good manners they managed to make me feel welcome without taking very much notice of me. Sometimes I glanced at the foreigners in the first class, and felt a little smugly that I was in better company than they were. Eventually Hydra came in sight, the once-so-familiar outline of the island making my heart go a little quicker. It's a long, grey, rather grim sight from the sea, like the back of a spiny lizard. Down the steep sides are reddish streaks where rocks have fallen away into the sea, like wounds in the side of the lizard.

Hydra is a strange island, and the wonder is that anybody even went to live there at all. There's hardly any water, and not much soil where you can grow anything. The islanders have a joke that when a man dies they have to bring soil from the mainland to bury him in. Originally the island was a stronghold for seafaring people, a place where pirates could hide out and, in the four centuries' Greek struggle against the occupying Turks, a place of heroes. The Turks never really got the measure of Hydra, and in the War of Independence great deeds were done by the Hydriot seamen. Afterwards they turned to commerce and the island is full of incongruously fine old houses built by the shipowners; but their day passed and when I first went to Hydra the islanders were grubbing a living by fishing for sponges. They had to sail in their small brightly-painted caïques all the way to North Africa for the sponges, and to dive for them so deep that they suffered from the water pressure, so that when I used to go there you would see cripples all the time, young men who had had the diver's sickness and would never walk straight again. They had stories to tell of fishing in those North African waters just after the war in places where the Malta convoys had gone down: a story I remember of a diver reaching to grasp a sponge from the ocean floor and finding it was a man's skull. They didn't make much money from those sponges, and the Hydra I knew was a desperately poor place. Out of the sponge season the divers used to make a little extra living from fishing in their home waters, often using dynamite left over from the war to save themselves the tedium of line and bait, and sometimes you'd meet a man with a hand or arm missing, who'd not let the dynamite go in time. A heroic place, then, a hard and poor place, and I wondered very much how it had changed with the influx of the foreigners and the making of those films and a measure of prosperity. It's a puzzle to know what to think about such matters: surely it must be good that poor people should become less poor, and yet so often when they do, they lose something that can't be valued in terms of money.

At first sight nothing had changed. The Hydra people are men of the sea who think of their town as a seaman thinks of his ship: as a thing to be cherished and kept spick and span. They keep their houses in paint like a ship, and families too poor to eat properly used to set aside money for a yearly repainting. They even used to paint the pavements round their houses. This hadn't changed. From the neck of the harbour the town looked neat as a pin. I felt I was home, and I clambered into the boat to be rowed ashore, thrilled by the old familiar sights and smells of the small harbour. That was the end of my content, though. As soon as I got ashore I might have been in Cannes or Saint Tropez or some horrible resort like that. The trippers were as thick as flies: Germans in their nasty leather shorts again, athletic crop-haired French boys, English girls with Kensington voices, blue-haired American matrons: everybody under the sun, but where were the Greeks? Well, I suppose they were there, rowing the boat that brought me from the ship, serving at the fish and vegetable stalls along the quay, waiters outside the café; but even the Hydriot fishermen with their nets suddenly looked like people in a play and the pretty painted houses like a stage set: the whole affair a sort of tableau set up for the holiday entertainment of the Kensington girls and the blue-haired Mommas.

I would have gone back to the boat, but I had a brainwave. I had noticed something about the tourists in Athens, how they kept to the beaten track, how they all went the same way, down certain streets, to certain cafés and bars, weaving, as it were, a safe tourists' maze of little rabbit tracks through the city that left everything else untouched. Surely they would do the same in Hydra, I thought. So I slung the knapsack I had taken with me and set off through the town, climbing up the steep streets away from the harbour. In a few minutes I was out in the country, clambering along a rocky path I found I remembered as if I'd been there yesterday. I knew where I was going. The sun shone down as strong as a blow, yet still bearable with that flawlessly blue sky and the crickets sawing away in the bushes and the faint smell of herbs and pine needles that's always in the air on a hot summer's day in the Greek countryside. I walked between olive trees as crooked as old crones, and beside a stream that babbled away like those gossiping voices in the third class on the ship. I knelt and drank some water that really tasted of water and picked and ate a prickly pear and got prickles in my hands and on my lips. I didn't mind at all. I passed a goat who gave me a moment's qualm when he lowered his head and sent me a sharp look from his baleful yellow eye. I climbed up and up the lizard's flank of Hydra, looking back once or twice at the pretty painted toy town below, the white church on a small island offshore, and the steamer now just a line of smoke on the horizon. On the spine of the lizard was a white windmill with tattered brown sails, and from there I would go down the other flank to a small ramshackle town by the shore, a cluster of houses not really a town, that was my destination. It's a little place that the Hydra people know about, where no foreigner ever goes. There I'd have my dinner and find somewhere to sleep.

As I passed the first couple of houses I heard the gentle murmur of greeting that you get everywhere in the countryside in Greece, 'Kalispera, Kalispera', and I Kalisperaed back. Old women were sitting in doorways, dressed in their usual black shrouds. A handsome girl was bashing some laundry on a stone by a waterbucket. A snotty little boy sat on a wall and regarded me with enormous eyes. An old man greeted me and a chicken squawked away from my feet. I was in the village square, if that was the word for a church and a little all-purpose shop and a taverna with some tables and chairs under a tree. I collared three of the chairs, rested an arm on one, and a leg on another, and sat on the third. This is the Greek way. No Greek can be comfortable on only one chair. A pleasant pockmarked youth arrived with a can of retsina and a couple of glasses. He knew it was safe to assume that in Greece you won't be drinking alone, or not for long. The retsina was cold from the cellar and I poured three glasses in quick succession. It was fine to be there by myself in the shade of the big tree, with the smell of pine needles and the sharp resin taste of the wine and the crickets singing. The village went about its desultory business of laundering and banging pots and pans. There would be an hour or so of this, I knew, before the sun went behind the hill. Then the men would come back from the fields or from their boats, and I would have company to share my drink with.

14
Italy: Venice Revealed
[September 1966]

I'VE been, I suppose, just about everywhere now, about eighty countries at the last count, but I seem to have missed quite a bit along the way. I don't know why, perhaps just lack of imagination or perhaps I didn't do my homework in the history class long ago, but I am the world's worst sightseer with the world's least active historical sense. I must be the only person who's set out on a two hundred mile long drive to see the Taj Mahal by moonlight and stopped by the way for a glass of tea (tea in India, not beer) and spent the rest of the night in that tea-house talking to the peasants instead of pushing on to the Taj. In London I've never been inside Westminster Abbey or the Tower of London, nor inside Notre Dame or the Louvre in Paris. On this trip round Europe I've missed half the sublime productions of European culture, preferring all too often to spend my time in coffee shops or bars or on park benches with new-found friends probably never to be seen again. I drove through Chartres a couple of months ago and didn't even *see* the Cathedral, which is quite a feat; and in Athens I failed to climb the Acropolis, though of course even I couldn't help seeing the thing stuck up there in the sky. Worse than all this, as far as I personally am concerned, is the fact that I don't take any pleasure or pride in my philistinism, indeed it makes me sad. So I decided something must be done about it before I ended this journey.

Well, I was going to Italy next, and that of course is the sightseer's country of countries, so I resolved to try my experiment of being a good sightseer there. There were plenty of candidates. Rome, I thought, would be too much for me and Florence too. I've been to these places before, and I thought I'd start my sightseeing a little less ambitiously. On the other hand places like Padua or Verona I turned down because I was afraid (with my blind sightseer's eye) I should find nothing to say about them. I thought wildly of Naples which I much prefer to any other Italian city, but of course Naples would be cheating, as it's a town with a lot of fascinating humanity but hardly any sights really. So my choice fell on Venice, where I hadn't been before, and there I flew one morning from Milan (another town splendidly without sights).

I had never been to Venice and I went armed with guidebooks and heaps of resolutions to be a good tourist for once. But we arrived out of a cloud and so I got no bird's-eye view to prepare me, and the launch from the airport chugged across the lagoon through a clammy mist so we might have been anywhere. I thumbed my guide book and stared at the map and waited for the great experience to arrive: the guide book had something about 'the finest constellation of beauty in all Europe'. Instead the first land that loomed out of the mist was San Michele, the island that serves as the city cemetery. I knew that Venice had always been a great place for dying: Wagner had died here, and Browning, and Diaghilev, and Baron Corvo; and I like cemeteries and thought I might allow myself an indulgent afternoon pottering among the graves on San Michele; but no, apparently: the guide informed me that land was scarce in Venice, and dead people couldn't be left to take up valuable space, so after ten years their bones are dug up and transferred to a public ossary (as it's called) on a neighbouring island. I just hoped this rough practice hadn't obtained in Wagner's day or Browning's. We chugged on into the mist and I caught a glimpse of some prefabricated blocks of flats on what seemed to be the island of St. Helena. I was beginning to feel faint-hearted already, but then we rounded the corner of St. Helena and suddenly, marvellously, the guide book came to life.

Here was 'the finest constellation of beauty in all Europe'. Perhaps I wouldn't have used quite *those* words, but the entrance to Venice from the sea side, with the church of San Giorgio on your left and the Piazza San Marco and the entrance to the Grand Canal dead ahead is about the most fabulous man-made thing I've ever seen.

It reminded me of my first confrontation with the Imperial City in Peking (one of the sights I *have* seen) which of course is totally unlike Venice but gives one the same impression of man's having made his mark pretty decisively. In Venice, of course, what was there before was a squalid mud-flat, and this approach from the sea is a wonderful way to get the hang of this extraordinary city, because the oddest thing about Venice is why is it there at all. What more inconvenient way of building a city can you imagine than to put it on the scattered mud islands of a swamp? Of course I know there were reasons of commerce and defence for this, but they could have been solved in other ways. It was human cussedness that built Venice thus, and as sometimes happens cussedness paid off triumphantly. The motor boat puttered in towards the silvery domes of St. Mark's and San Giorgio and now also the Salute and as we drew nearer to the mouth of the Grand Canal we saw our first gondolas, their long lop-sided black hulks with the curious six-pronged steel blade at the prow. The gondolas themselves are still being built new, but the design is centuries-tried and stays much the same. Even the gondoliers are of the same breed because it is a skilful trade and a closed one; but what has changed is the people they carry, and the first one we passed had four members of some visiting American convention on board, identifiable by their straw boaters and a large plastic identity badge on each lapel. We drew in to the quay, and the guide book spoke to me again, rather beguilingly. The air terminal was decorated with the usual crude airline posters, but apparently it had been built originally by Napoleon, who liked to take his coffee there as he surveyed his new, but temporary conquest. Next door was Harry's American Bar, familiar to readers of Hemingway and I suppose to every American visitor to Venice, and the steps of Harry's Bar before Harry's day was where Baron Corvo, the wretched Frederick Rolfe, slept during his last weeks in Venice when his most unhappy of lives had at last brought him to destitution. Nobody knew Corvo then; today even the denizens of Harry's Bar might be prepared to buy him a drink.

I left my bags at a pensione and started off on my attempt to 'do' Venice. It was only a pensione, and not the Palazzo Danieli, of which Ruskin said that 'the beginning of all my visits is in seeing the beak of the gondola come inside the door at Danieli's, when the tide is up and the water two feet deep at the foot of the stairs'. The

Danieli is still a hotel, but thanks to people like the convention men, out of *my* reach; but the water is as deep as ever, indeed deeper, and the news is that the whole city is slowly sinking into the sea, and Venice as she is is with us for hardly more than another hundred years.

The American humourist Robert Benchley when he came here cabled home in a pretended panic: 'Streets Full of Water: What To Do?' and the fact that the streets *are* full of water is the obvious but still the most surprising thing about this strange city (that, and the equally engaging fact that they are *not* full of cars). I was amazed during my few days in Venice never to see anyone fall into the canals. I had imagined continual disasters of this kind, and the graveyard at San Michele crammed with the corpses of drunkards and little children, but apparently it hardly ever happens and in any case the Grand Canal is only nine feet deep and the side ones only about the depth of a bath tub. Now *that's* the kind of fact *I* find more interesting than the deaths of kings and the attribution of famous paintings, but I told myself that was *not* why I had come to Venice. I *could* tell you, for instance, exactly how they get rid of the sewage in Venice, but I shall proceed directly to the serious business of St. Mark's Square. Napoleon called this the largest drawing-room in Europe, and you can see what he meant: how in spite of its splendour there is a human dimension in all the buildings, in the colonnades and towers, that is almost domestic. Alas it has now turned into the largest museum-room in Europe, and none of the gaping crowds, including those Americans and myself, would have been much at home in Napoleon's drawing-room. Every tourist in St. Mark's except myself seemed to be part of a guided party, and I shamelessly attached myself to several of these parties in turn, comparing the various versions of history and architecture the English-speaking guides handed out to their flocks. The versions did not agree, but nobody protested. I suppose they were listening. I was listening, but then, being ignorant, I was in no position to protest, even if I had paid for the privilege, so I shall never know whether the columns in front of the Doge's palace once had bases or not or whether the capitals of the columns are the original ones. I suppose I could easily have found out, but already my resolution was beginning to wane. I was determined to get to the top of the Campanile, the famous tower, before that resolution went altogether. I'm told it was once possible to ride a horse up a sloping ramp to the top, which would have been nice, but today the journey is by a convenient and unhistorical lift.

At the top you can indeed (as the guide book says) 'hold Venice in the palm of your hand', and the sight was an instructive one. I don't only mean that you could see the exact layout of the small, strange city: where the Grand Canal wound, where the famous churches were, and the outlines of the islands in the lagoon. You could also see two separate Venices: one the Venice of the guide book, of the tourists, where the neon signs and the pavement canopies of the restaurants lay side by side with the churches and the monuments; the other, and, oh, to me so much more attractive, a messy blotchy-coloured Italian town of winding streets and small neglected canals where the Venetians lived. As in other places, I was struck by the very small area the visitors had colonized: a few streets, a few squares, the Grand Canal but very few of the side canals, and of course beyond the lagoon the Lido where there was a Film Festival going on which wild sea-horses would not have dragged me to. The rest of the city was not less old—or, to my mind, much less beautiful, and there I decided, looking down from the Campanile, I would go, in betrayal of all my resolutions.

Down from the tower, I got out the guide book and started off along one of the standard routes. Whimsically, perhaps, I would let Venice guide my footsteps away from her own past. Past the Bridge of Sighs I went (such a small bridge for so much fuss), past the stalls for postcards and trinkets and the shops selling hideous Venetian glass, past the Scuola di San Giorgio where there were paintings to be seen but I did not go in, through some winding streets and past the prison, from which Casanova once escaped, a building of truly mediaeval horribleness, and past the Danieli Hotel, where Ruskin and his wife stayed and played Battledore and Shuttlecock and Alfred de Musset and his mistress, George Sand, stayed and didn't get anywhere either, and on again past the church in the Campo Santa Maria Formosa about which Ruskin wrote some of his most overdone descriptions and now I was getting into a world I felt more at home in: indeed the Italian world I might have found in somewhere like Naples if I had gone the whole hog from the start: a world of women with broad hips hanging out washing, and children with bare feet rushing out of alleys, screaming with excitement at some incomprehensible game, and old men who hadn't had a shave for a week drinking wine at café tables or smoking on their doorsteps. It was a world of beggars, the beggars the authorities have cleared off the tourist streets of Venice, a world of poverty, and ignorance I am sure, but there was a sense in which this was the real world of Venice, which even Ruskin and Browning and Wagner and all those other expatriates would have recognized as a Venice they knew. Certainly someone like Corvo, who sank to the dregs, or Byron, who tasted the dregs by choice, would have felt at home here; while the official Venice of the painters and the sculptors and the great Princes who employed them in the days when Venice was great had become just a museum for tourists such as myself to gape at. I was sorry at losing my resolution, but glad that I had changed my mind.

15
France : In Search of Wild Horses
[October 1966]

THIS journey I made in France a couple of weeks ago had its beginnings nearly thirty years before in Africa. Let me explain. I was a schoolboy in Capetown of about ten or eleven, and I had just found out that such a thing as poetry existed. From the start I could see what fun poetry was, even in the rather awful anthology we had at school, but there were unexpected difficulties in reading English poetry for an African child who had never seen England. Most of the poems in that anthology were about disappointed love (which I wasn't quite ready for yet) or else about the English countryside, and the English countryside couldn't be more different from the South African countryside. The sound of the poems was fine, especially the more rollicking ones, but what were we colonial children to make of these daffodils, hedgerows, blackberries and mayflowers that came in every second poem and that all of Europe was apparently stuffed with? None of the poets ever seemed to mention thorn trees, or cactus, or mealie plants, or mimosa or prickly pears, which were all we knew. The weather and the animals, the whole of nature in fact, in those poems from Europe was altogether different from our own, and we assumed sadly and enviously that anything like a South African poet was an impossibility; assumed this, that is, until the great day when someone found an anthology with a poem by Roy Campbell in it.

By some miracle he was actually a South African, and his poem described a place that surely we had seen for ourselves. I've known the poem by heart ever since, and it begins:

'In the grey wastes of dread,
The haunt of shattered gulls where nothing moves
But in a shroud of silence like the dead,
I heard a sudden harmony of hooves,
And, turning, saw afar
A hundred snowy horses unconfined,
The silver runaways of Neptune's car
Racing, spray-curled, like waves before the wind.'

The whole scene was something I could easily identify: the grey wastes of the Cape Flats, the haunted empty sands under Table Mountain where riding horses from the stables of the rich Capetown whites are exercised by ragged Cape Coloured grooms. There one misty morning I had seen a flock of these horses galloping along the sands and one in particular, a snowy-coloured horse with a grey mane, had raced before the wind with a special recklessness. I felt as if I had written Roy Campbell's poem myself, but there was just one thing that didn't fit. The poem continues:

'Sons of the Mistral, fleet
As him with whose strong gusts they love to flee,'

and of course the Mistral is *not* the South-Wester of Capetown but the wind that blows down the Rhône Valley to the Mediterranean coast of France, and the title of Roy Campbell's poem is 'Horses on the Camargue', the famous wild horses of that mysterious corner of Europe, the triangle of dead flat waste land that forms the delta of the Rhône. In the months that followed I learned as much as I could about the Camargue in the Capetown Public Library and resolved quite deliberately that one day I would go there and see if it did look just like the Cape Flats and see the wild white horses for myself.

I arrived in Avignon with that small excited feeling in the pit of my stomach that is one of the nicest feelings there is. Avignon was on my way to the Camargue, but I've always been rather put off it by the song—you know, the one about the bridge—and I was afraid the place would be too touristy and I wasn't wrong. I like my ruins to be a little ruined, and Avignon is far too spick and span. The Popes departed six hundred years ago, after using Avignon as a Vatican for a while, but the Palace of the Popes looks as well preserved as though they'd moved out yesterday. The ruined bridge looks as if it was built ruined, like a film set; and at night bridge, palace and ramparts are illuminated for the *Son et Lumière*, whose loudspeakers make the town hideous with actors bellowing historical dialogue which sounds like a recording of a Home Service schools programme on a very off day. Far more to my taste were a couple of live minstrels who played on the guitar and sang under the plane trees outside the restaurants of the Place de l'Horloge. I looked at their dark faces and thought I was back in Greece, but I'd heard you can often see these faces in Provence, the heirs of Greek colonists who came here two thousand years ago. The minstrels had a gipsy wildness about them and spoke and sang in the strange accent of Provence, very sing-song and full of twanging sounds, like a man with his mouth full of rubber bands.

It was time to press on and the next morning I took the bus through Tarascon, with its huge castle that leans over the road as if it were just about to tumble into the traffic, and along the Rhône—where the current is so fast that it twists the water into ropes—down to Arles, which is where the Camargue really begins.

Driving into Arles the visitor gets the strangest feeling as if he's been there before, and if he's as forgetful as I am it may be an hour or two before he realizes that of course he has been here before, in the paintings of Van Gogh. The fields outside Arles are his, and the fiery sun is his and on the day I arrived in Arles not in the least exaggerated, and the faces of the people in the rough café where I waited to catch my connection to the Camargue were the stubby, creased faces of Van Gogh's café scenes. I chatted to some of these fellows, and helped by them, making the best I could of the strange twanging sounds, I worked out a plan. The best thing seemed to be to go straight across the Camargue to Les Saintes Maries de la Mer and then on my feet to search the marshes for my wild white horses. I asked about the horses and found great approval for my quest. Everybody wanted to talk about them. There is a great mythology about these horses. Nobody is sure where they come from: some say they came with the Saracen invaders, others that they are of Mongol stock. They are brave and intelligent, my informants said, many of them still roam wild but they are gentle and not shy when you approach them. They are small, they said, but they have enormous feet, because the Southern Camargue is all sand and marshes. They are as happy in the water as on land. One man in the group kept on saying something I couldn't make out and fooling with his moustache, until another man translated: 'He says the horses have moustaches.'

'I beg your pardon?'

'Yes, they have moustaches. They have tried to breed this out, but the *chevaux blancs* are very stubborn. Nearly all of them have moustaches.' Roy Campbell had mentioned nothing about this.

The bus carried me off and for some time there was no particular sign we were in the Camargue. The grimy suburbs of Arles were succeeded by an odd scene that might have been in South East Asia: paddy fields of rice growing up to its ears in water, the water gleaming in the sun like mirrors, just as it does in Vietnam and Cambodia, where the French learned the rice cultivation which will one day cover the whole of the Camargue. About half way to the coast a bleakness came over the land, and the wind, instead of rippling the water of the paddy fields, began to scuff up spirals of sand and ruffle the coarse marsh grass which grows here. The Camargue began to live up to the picture Roy Campbell had created in my mind so many years before, as a piece of Europe that even an African could understand:

> '. . . the grey wastes of dread,
> The haunt of shattered gulls where nothing moves.'

And then I saw my first white horse. He wasn't wild, but instead was being ridden by the most splendidly authentic-looking cowboy. He had old-fashioned heavy stirrups and a real Western saddle with a high front and back and wore a cowboy hat and tattered old leather trousers. To improve his image even further, he was driving not a herd of cows but a bunch of the most frightening bulls I've ever seen. This man was one of the *gardiens*, a cowboy of the Camargue on his white horse, caught wild and broken in, and he was driving his *manade*, or herd of black fighting bulls. These bulls are raised purely for fighting, and every farm in the Camargue has a field or two with a notice on the fence: '*Attention: Torres de Combat*.'

We soon reached Les Saintes Maries, and I was disappointed by the smart cafés and the holiday-makers in shorts, but pleased to see a bull-fight arena in the centre of town, and being a Saturday there was a bull-fight today. In the bull-fights of the Camargue they don't kill the bull or even hurt him: the most they do is give him some exercise. No bull has ever been hurt in one of these romps, which didn't stop the whole village from crowding into the small arena. A loudspeaker whistled, and flags flew round the place: any flags they happened to have handy I noticed, including the Union Jack, the Swiss flag, and the flag of a well-known French aperitif manufacturer. The bull-fight consisted of half a dozen young men trying to snatch a sort of posy or rosette off the left horn of a succession of bulls. They shouted at the bull, pulled faces at him, barked like dogs or neighed like horses, and then when he charged furiously they would make a grab for the rosette and then leap for dear life over the barrier. All great fun, but for me the great attraction of the afternoon was a marvellous exhibition of the cowboys riding white horses bareback, jumping from one to another as they galloped full tilt round the ring. This was almost what I had come for, but not quite. Perhaps tomorrow would bring that. In the bar between contests I made myself a nuisance with my map of the Camargue, asking which were the wildest parts of the marshes, where there would be no tourists and a chance of seeing the wild horses. I picked a walk of about fifteen miles across part of the marshes furthest from the roads and started out early next morning. I hurried out of town past the shiny hotel and Kiki's Stable Bar and the Sheriff's Discothèque, but as soon as the road became rough enough these horrors were left behind, and I was alone with the silence of the Camargue.

Living in towns or near roads as most of us in Europe do, we have almost forgotten what silence is. I stopped for a moment on the path and unexpectedly had a feeling of astonishment. Why was I astonished? Simply because I could hear absolutely nothing. Then there was one very small sound, and that was the wind in the marsh grasses, and another hardly louder and that was a seagull, far away over the salt flats. Otherwise for long periods there was nothing to hear or see as I walked along. Just occasionally there would be a flight of storks against the sky, or I would pass one of the curious little reed huts where the cowboys sometimes spend a night. A stuffy sort of smell came from the marshes and reddish dragonflies hovered beside the path like tiny helicopters. There were pieces of driftwood white as bone, twisted into strangely human shapes. As I got further into the marshes there was more life: rabbits leaping out almost from under my feet, and once I glanced into a rabbit hole near my feet and saw a little gleam where the rabbit was looking back at me. It was the very best of mornings, and I wandered on, not minding the growing heat or the mosquitoes that infest the Camargue in autumn. There was something nice and surprising to see every few minutes, but so far not the most important thing of all: the white horses. Where were the wild horses? And then I saw them. At first I thought I must have wandered on to someone's farm, because they were standing so tamely there, about a quarter of a mile away, but there were no fences and there wasn't a farm. Somehow I expected the horses to be galloping across the landscape as wild as the apocalypse. Instead they were standing around in a small hollow keeping each other company, not a hundred but about twenty, counting a few foals. The mares and stallions were white or whitish, the foals brown, so dark brown that they seemed a different breed. None of them took any notice of me, and I crept as close as I dared, perhaps fifty yards, and there I sat for an hour, while the mosquitoes made a meal of me, watching the wild white horses nuzzling, and feeding, and waving their tails unceasingly to keep off the mosquitoes, until slowly they drifted away towards the sea, and I didn't follow them but let them go; because I'd kept my promise to myself now, I'd been to 'the grey wastes of dread', and seen 'the white horses of the windy plain', the white horses of the Camargue.

16
Spain : What Next?
[October 1966]

As I came into the dining car on the train from Barcelona to Madrid, I looked around quickly to see who I would choose as a table companion. I wanted someone I could talk to—and a Spaniard, not a tourist like myself—but the problem was I don't know Spanish. I chose a young man who certainly looked Spanish, for one thing he was too neatly dressed, combed and shaved to be one of us, and he looked like a student because he was reading a book, and because he was a student there was a chance he knew English.

I sat down opposite him and we began what turned out to be a long conversation. He was a law student and therefore a good person to choose as one's first person to talk to in Spain, because the law in Spain, I knew, isn't just something you study if you want to be a lawyer. It's the school for every ambitious young man, who wants to go into politics, or to be a writer, or a business tycoon, or go into the civil service or even the army, and I was lucky with my young man. A torrent of talk poured out of him, and before very long we were talking about politics, though I was careful about bringing politics up, because as we know Spain is a country with no politics, a dictatorship where Opposition is not just an abstract noun but the name of a criminal offence. My young man was extremely intelligent, and free-spoken to a degree that amazed me; but two things stood out above all as he spoke: firstly the extraordinary naïvety of his political ideas, and secondly, the fact that he was perfectly aware of this and very bitter about it. 'In Spain,' he said, 'we are children who do not know how to think. And we do not know how to think, because we are always treated like children.' And he went on to talk about what young Spaniards are like today. 'Most of my friends,' he said, 'are perfectly happy. They are quite content to have other people make up their minds for them. If they read in the government press that such and such a regulation concerning the university has been passed they feel no sense of grievance that they are not consulted and that their compliance is taken entirely for granted.'

These are the great majority of students, of young people generally, who are interested only in cars and clothes and pop groups and in getting a well-paid job with plenty of security after graduation. This is the typical young Spaniard, my young friend in the dining car said—tamed, not as foreigners like myself tend to assume, by despotism and dictatorship but by the blandishments of comfort and security that tame young people everywhere in the world. Well, all right, they are perfectly happy, I said, but what about you, and then my student friend began to tell me about his frustration and those of people like him and voiced his complaint about being a child who had never been allowed to think for himself. What he was saying was perfectly true. People can't think straight if they never get any practice at thinking, and if they live in a country where thinking aloud is sometimes a dangerous business. I asked about the new liberal measures I had heard about, raising press censorship and allowing more open political debate. My young friend was scornful. Grousing, he explained, is all right in Spain, and always has been. Spaniards are great grousers. If you want to sit in the local cantina and grumble over your glass of brandy about the rise in prices, the cost of an apartment, the bad roads, the corruption of Ministers, even the corruption of a particular Minister, that is perfectly all right. No one is going to report you to the secret police. What the regime can't stand is any constructive discussion which envisages a different system to the present one. As for lifting the press censorship, he continued, they soon clamp it back on if the papers dare to print anything that really says anything. 'And this brings us to the point,' he went on, 'that this is the time when Spaniards should be thinking for themselves, because the day will come soon when we have to decide: when Spain will have to say: What next?'

What comes after Franco? For nearly thirty years since the end of the Civil War the country has been in a deep sleep from which it's only beginning to awake. In the last few years the new prosperity brought by the tourists and by well-timed American aid has lifted the country at least part way out of the wretchedness that came with the Civil War; but still very little progress has been taken towards making that decision: What next? There are various possibilities, and I spent my week in Madrid trying to find out what they were and how strong. Again I was surprised at how freely people talked. Yet behind the talk was the same aimlessness and helplessness which the student in the train expressed: the same feeling that however the outcome might be discussed, ordinary people would have no say in what actually happened. What sort of government would follow Franco's dictatorship? Would it be a republic, or a monarchy? Would it be another dictatorship, or some sort of democracy; and if a democracy, one of the left or the right? It was easy enough to find out what the factors were, impossible to be sure how they would combine in the end.

For instance, there is the role of the Army. Spain is perhaps the only European country where the Army has the same importance it has in countries like Egypt or Pakistan. Whoever rules in Spain must command the Army's loyalty. It's an Army of about a hundred and eighty thousand with an abnormally high proportion of officers, about thirty thousand, and a ridiculously high number of generals, about two hundred. In the years after the Civil War the Army was of course a very great power in the land, and indeed they looked on themselves as the victors of a Holy Crusade in which the anti-Christ of International Communism had been defeated. It's among these people that some of the strongest advocates of what is called 'Continuismo' are found, the philosophy held by people who have prospered under the present regime and devoutly wish for its perpetuation, probably in the form of an Army-supported government but with a monarch to lend respectability and stability. A lot of wealthy Spaniards have got their fortunes by syphoning off government funds and other forms of corruption, but corruption is a hard thing to define in a country like Spain. How is one to regard the practice of appointing generals in the Army to positions on the boards of state-controlled industrial enterprises? Their military salaries are low, perhaps seventy pounds a month, but their pay as directors is liable to make this up to seven hundred pounds. Perhaps they are worth seven hundred pounds a month for their two jobs, but a man who is getting seven hundred pounds a month from the government is likely to be that government's most loyal supporter. Thus may General Franco be said to have bought the Army without a dishonest penny changing hands and after his death the generals at least will be passionately for maintaining the *status quo*. For many years the Army had no links whatsoever with even mildly leftist elements in Spanish life, but among the younger officers this situation is changing and a good many are in favour of a republic.

This brings one to the question of a monarchy in the future, or a republic. It isn't likely that a Spanish government of a left-wing cast would invite either Don Juan or his son Juan Carlos to assume the throne, and Spain would then become a republic again. The whole question of the restoration of the monarchy is a very tricky one. On this matter the people I talked to in Madrid were vaguer than ever. Spain actually is a monarchy already, has been technically since 1947, but Franco probably has no intention of letting anyone push him out of the limelight while he still draws breath. From my conversations with Spaniards I could get no very clear idea of how much they wanted a king again. Both Don Juan and Juan Carlos are regarded with respect and affection, and indeed over the years they have behaved with tact and with a patriotism that Spaniards particularly admire. And there's one factor that even more than respect or affection might bring Don Juan or Juan Carlos back to the throne; and that is what I've sensed among the Spaniards (I may be wrong) as a kind of fear of freedom, a need they feel for a father figure, for a strong figure at the centre of things, who will hold the country together and save them from their own ungovernable impulses towards anarchy and destruction. This is a feeling that Franco has been able to exploit, and it's a feeling that would ensure a great deal of support for the monarchy when Franco dies. Yet the signs are there that to a great many Spaniards who want their country at last to make that giant and necessary step into the twentieth century, nothing will do except some kind of republic with all the freedoms they have been denied by Franco, a republic probably with a mildly socialist government.

Although the students my friend in the train was telling me about seem so complacent, and a recent poll showed that seventy-seven per cent of Spanish students are not interested in politics, remember that means that twenty-three per cent are, and that's probably enough. Only last week students were demonstrating in Barcelona, and being beaten up by the police. Then there are the young priests, inspired by Pope John and the Vatican Council, who seem to be starting a wind of change in the Church. And there is that most potent force, the million or so Spanish workers who have gone to work in Germany, France or Switzerland and who are sending home ideas as well as money. These inhabitants of a Trojan Horse in reverse will have something to say for themselves in a year or two. And there is the Spanish working class in Spain, the rebellious Asturian miners and the country people who are flocking to the cities, traditionally a force that brings change. It may seem that this all adds up to a headache for Franco himself, but I don't think so.

The popularity of Franco is quite extraordinary. A Madrid editor who loathes the mention of his name told me he was quite convinced that in a free national popularity poll Franco would get seventy per cent of the votes. If you hear his Ministers and his police criticized in every cantina, you never seem to hear a word said against him. For a dictator who has put so many people in jail, it's extraordinary that in thirty years among the passionate Spanish not a single attempt has been made on his life. He is known to be personally incorruptible, and his ideals for Spain can be compared to those of General de Gaulle for France. His powers are even more extraordinary. In no other country of the world is there a leader who personally appoints all his cabinet ministers. As a statesman he has been underrated. His main aim at the moment is to get into the Common Market. So far Spain has been excluded because of her undemocratic failings like the censorship, but by subtle concessions from Franco which in fact concede very little, I am sure Spain will be in the Common Market before Britain is.

Franco's handling of the Gibraltar affair has been most skilful. Although Spain has no rights that any logical person would concede, Franco has contrived to make Britain appear in the wrong, or at least to make it seem that there is a case for us to answer. Unfortunately this very remarkable man has one failing that we all have; he is not immortal, though he seems inclined to believe that he is. Not long ago he boasted to a journalist friend of mine in Madrid that his father had lived to be ninety-three, while his grandfather had reached his century. In fact Franco himself is seventy-three and said not to be as spry as he once was. It's so difficult to weigh up the rumours that gather round a man like him, but it's obvious that he can't go on for ever. Spaniards want to know what is going to happen next, and by his suppression of their political instincts Franco has deprived them of the ability to decide for themselves. What is going to happen now will probably be decided for them. Well, let us hope the decision doesn't come too late, because the last time the Spaniards got in a muddle we remember what happened.

17
Thoughts After Europe
[October 1966]

WE'VE been talking about 'Going into Europe' for so long that the whole idea is in danger of becoming one of those British bores, like 'Shall We Build the Channel Tunnel?' or 'Should There Be Sunday Sport?' or 'What About the Licensing Laws?' What do the Europeans, though, think about us 'Going into Europe'? I spent the summer this year travelling through sixteen European countries in three months, from Finland to Spain, and Poland to France, talking to many hundreds of people, and not very often did the subject even come up, unless I dragged it in. The sad fact is that the Europeans in general don't think of Britain very much at all, and when they do, not necessarily in a very complimentary way. The Europeans already in the Common Market believe, I think (of course I am generalizing), that we never will go into the European Community, or if we try to we'll leave it so late that they won't let us in. In dozens of conversations with every sort of person—German businessmen, Italian students, French shopkeepers—I heard again and again the complaint, occasionally expressed not very politely, that we are trying to have our cake and eat it; that we are hopelessly attached to outworn dreams of imperial grandeur, and the sad image of the lion with his head buried in the sand was the commonly held view of us and one I saw frequently in cartoons.

This is a fairly new attitude in Europe towards Britain. When I first travelled in Europe immediately after the war, and for many years after that, it was quite something to be British, and kindnesses and favours came your way that wouldn't have if you were French or German, and certainly not if you were American. This is so no longer, though people are still immensely helpful nearly everywhere, certainly much more so than they are on the average in bored and indifferent Britain. Sometimes this kindness to the stranger, especially from an older person, seemed to be out of a sentimental gratitude for that long-ago time in the 1940s when Britain undoubtedly saved Europe. When I talk of that time as long ago and the emotion as sentimental I may offend people who have very good reason to remember that time; but let us remember that nearly one third of the population of Europe is under twenty-one and they have no personal reason to be grateful to Britain, while perhaps another quarter were very small children during the war who had a difficult time making their way among the ruins of post-war Europe.

To the great majority of these people Britain seems to have contributed little or nothing to Europe since the war, and two things follow from this: firstly, that the Europeans are resentful about what they see as our selfishness, and (being human) aren't altogether sorry to see us in our present predicaments; and secondly, that we have lost great opportunities. Contrast us with the Americans. They not only did a tremendous amount to put Europe on her feet after the war; they were sensible enough to cash in on their own good deeds. Today American investment in European industry is almost impossible to calculate, and indeed many European ears would burn if the total were known. A most remarkable city to visit is Geneva. Now, of course, Switzerland has many advantages for the investor who wants to speculate in Europe and still keep his money as safe as possible. As a result Geneva is the headquarters of dozens of American corporations; glance at the Geneva telephone book and you wonder for a moment what country you are in, there is such a mixture of names. Throughout Western Europe, I would say the most favoured and admired country, the one that many people even prefer to their own, is the United States; and there is one sad consequence of this: and that's the extraordinary uniformity of Europe today. A favourite game of mine was to look out from the window of a train or the terrace of a café, eliminate anything written up like an advertisement that would give away the language of the country, and then try and work out what country I was in. It wasn't always possible to tell.

To an extraordinary degree everyone in Western Europe wears the same clothes, drives the same cars, looks at the same television programmes, sees the same films, takes their holidays or inclusive tours in the same places, has the same ambitions (for a colour supplement style house or apartment, a second car, even more modish clothes, colour television, more expensive holidays). This is all extremely depressing, not because these are depressing ambitions in themselves, though I find them so, but because the whole scene is so second-rate; Europe isn't Europe any more, but a second-rate version of America. Drive through a recently built suburb in Frankfurt or Stockholm, or Helsinki, or Milan, or Zurich, and you might be in the suburbs of New York or Boston, except that in America the buildings are more stylish, the landscaping more imaginative, the cars shinier. Of course I am flying a kite here, and there *is* plenty of the old Europe still to be seen, but even that is taking on the semblance of an open air museum and the inhabitants often seem to be like film extras, obligingly playing the parts of Europeans for Americans and other Europeans to gape at. Now I have the greatest admiration for America and many things American, but if that sort of life were my personal preference I should get on a plane and fly Westwards as quickly as possible, rather than stay in the American slum that much of Europe is becoming.

Of course up to now I have mentioned only one Europe, the Europe I saw in Finland and Sweden, saw again in Austria and Northern Italy and Switzerland and France and Belgium and Western Germany and West Berlin. There was another Europe I visited as well: the Europe I saw when I went with Finnish friends on a trip to Esthonia, the Europe of Poland today and Czechoslovakia and Yugoslavia, and the non-communist but on the surface not-so-different worlds of Greece and Spain. Nowhere of course do you see the contrast more strikingly than in Berlin.

I have always had a soft spot for East Berlin, and felt that people were too easily put off by the shabby appearance of the place; but for a long time there was no doubt that West Berlin was more fun, had more interesting people to see and lively things to do. Now I'm not so sure. In the first ten years after the war, in West Berlin, it was a brave sight to see the horrifying acres of rubble tidied up and new buildings going up, tall glass American boxes in the wilderness. The people were a gutsy lot too, who refused to decamp to West

Germany though what with the Air Lift and the East Berlin Uprising and the events that led to the Wall they were not exactly in a comfortable position. The East on the other hand was pretty depressing, with the grim barracks of the Stalinallee apartment buildings rising amid the ruins. At first one wondered why they didn't take the trouble to clean the place up a bit. Quite apart from politics, the sheer gloom of the surroundings must have sent quite a few people over to the West. Well, it appears the East Germans had their reasons, and returning a couple of months ago I had a big surprise. My last few visits to Berlin had been hurried and in winter when the place on both sides of the Wall always looks pretty gloomy. This time it was a week of bright sunshine, with the girls bathing in the Wannsee and rabbits skipping through the barbed wire along the Wall. I got a car and drove all over West Berlin, in increasing gloom at what I now saw was the hideousness of the place. The nearest thing I could think of was somewhere like Jersey City or, nearer home, one of the modern cities of West Germany, Stuttgart or Frankfurt or Düsseldorf. All the new buildings were modern and made of glass, of course, but there is modern and modern and these had been put up with an unprincipled eye for opportunity.

The city wasn't a city, just a twentieth-century slum, a machine for making money, built by chancers from West Germany taking advantages of the special concessions that industry and property development can command in West Berlin. There was nothing German about the place: that's the point. Then I went over to the East, and of course there are still heaps of unmended or half-mended houses, but there is also something new, a few streets and avenues that would grace any capital city. Here are the old buildings of the Unter den Linden and the Alexanderplatz area painstakingly restored, clean and tidy in green gardens along straight avenues. Buildings like these where they existed in West Berlin were pulled down as being too much trouble to repair, and in East Berlin: well, there were the Russian reparations to pay and then new industry to build up, so it was a matter of first things first and only lately have the East Berliners been able to start putting the city together again. When they've finished the job I hope I see it; and I'd also like to see the greedy faces of the West Berlin City fathers who put money before patriotism. Not that I think much of patriotism as a rule, but the Germans do, they are the most nationalistic people in Europe as we well know, and when they cast eyes on their new capital city, looking so German, standing next to that New Jersey slum on the other side of the wall, well, I think German unification will take a huge leap forward. I'm not saying this will be good in itself, only that I was glad to have the opportunity to see something European on my journey through Europe. In fact the countries of the Eastern Bloc are altogether more European than the rest, and I found them, as I always do, a most refreshing change from the sad and greedy values of the Affluent Societies of the West, though I'm only too aware that their own values have a pretty sad side.

The traveller in Eastern Europe is placed in a tricky position. On the one hand it's delightful to find a society with a real sense of its past in spite of indoctrination; cities which look like cities and not just the suburbs of a single vast international cosmopolis; their streets not filled with cars and the countryside not made hideous by advertisements; and people who have to stick to fairly simple things, who are not hemmed off from life by a hunger for possessions and a desire to keep up with the neighbours. But of course one has to realise, what was made very plain to me by my East European friends, that very many of them want exactly these things. Young Polish students cut the food and drink advertisements out of American magazines when they can get them and put them up in their studies as pin-ups; and everybody in Eastern Europe wants a car, it's no good telling them what hell the motor car is in process of turning our lives into; and once they start getting these things they'll want more.

I found some East Europeans who believed they were building a fairer society, and in some ways I think theirs is a fairer society, certainly it's a less silly one. Their ideals may be subject to the human compromises, cruelties and corruption that all ideals are, but still they have some ideals and it would be a bold or foolish man who asserted that we have anything much left of that kind in Western Europe. There is another reason why I find life in Eastern Europe attractive, and it's a painful one to confess to. Journalists are not really honest men. We are like the Comedians that Graham Greene wrote about in his recent novel: people who never really get involved in anything, voyeurs of other people's lives. In a few weeks I am going to Vietnam, I shall no doubt get opportunities to write at first hand about the horribleness of war; but in a further few weeks I shall be back snug in London while the people actually fighting the war, and having it fought round them, will still be there, and wishing they weren't.

So with Eastern Europe. What makes life exciting there for a visitor like myself is a sense that this is a serious place where people are up against it, a place where telephones are tapped and men in plain clothes sometimes beat on doors in the night. This puts an edge on the people who live there, so they are simply more interesting to know than the fortunate folk of Western Europe with their swinging lives, their colour supplements and their motor shows and inclusive tour holidays and all the rest. But then, as I say, the visitor like myself is sometimes just a voyeur of their suffering, a man who isn't involved, and to be a voyeur of men in plain clothes beating on doors in the night is a pretty horrible thing, so I suppose that the other life is better, this other fortunate life of ours; and we in Western Europe had better try and make the best of the air-conditioned daydream in which we find ourselves.

PART THREE

AFRICA

18

Ethiopia : Journey to Harar
[January 1962]

JUST about the first thing I did after arriving in Ethiopia was to arrange to leave the country as soon as possible. I'd flown in to Addis Ababa from Cairo; now I wanted to fly out again, down to Djibouti in French Somaliland on the Red Sea coast. I had a reason for this fickle behaviour. Just before leaving London I'd come across the following splendid short telegram in *The Times*: 'Addis Ababa. It is reported that armed robbers derailed the Djibouti-Addis Ababa express last night by placing boulders on the track. In the mêlée that followed, the robbers took all the passengers' money, luggage and clothing before fleeing into the desert darkness.' This was the stuff. How I should like to have witnessed the arrival of a trainload of naked passengers.

This wasn't the first I had heard of this remarkable railway. If you've read the hilarious books by Evelyn Waugh about Ethiopia, you'll remember it. I wondered whether the engine-driver still blazed away at wild animals with his ancient muzzle-loader; and whether we would stop at dusk to eat fine French cooking in a candle-lit tent pitched beside the tracks. The Djibouti railway was obviously the true gateway to Ethiopia and I would have to travel on it. So as soon as I made my first (and, as it were, unofficial) entrance into Addis, I set about trying to get down to Djibouti, so as to make this important journey in the right direction.

I needed a plane, and there was no regular passenger service, only a daily cargo flight, and when I asked about this in Addis, people tended to be mysterious. 'Oh, that's the "chat"-flight,' they said in a slightly embarrassed way. 'The what?' 'The "chat"-flight.' What was that? It turned out that of the few humble exports the Ethiopians have, perhaps the chief is a drug, a weed called 'chat'. It's a sort of poor relation of hashish or marijuana, and it grows in the hills around the old walled city of Harar. The Arabs of the Red Sea coast are addicted to chat. They chew it, just as it is, rather as you might chew a laurel bush. It makes them excited. Every day an aircraft flew down from Addis to Dire Dawa near Harar to pick up the chat; then on to Djibouti. The airline said they would take me, but I would be the only passenger, in an aircraft otherwise full of weeds.

I expected the chat would be piled like hay, but no, they loaded it into the plane in hundreds of little parcels wrapped in sacking. The pilot gave me one for myself, presumably to chew on the journey. (I was relieved to see he wasn't having any himself.) To my surprise the parcel was hot. Apparently chat wrapped in parcels is prone to spontaneous combustion, just the thing to carry in an aeroplane. As we flew over the barren desert of French Somaliland, bald as a parade ground, I nibbled at the leaves. There was a suggestion of the smoky cloying taste of hashish, but on the whole they tasted just like green leaves. There was no effect. I was far more excited by looking out of the window, and seeing what could be nothing but the great Djibouti railway winding through the flat brown desert below. It seemed to wind more than it need, considering there was nothing in the way.

At Djibouti there was a brief glimpse of the intensely blue Red Sea, and then we landed in the desert, having arrived apparently nowhere. We climbed down, and there was nothing to see: just a couple of huts, a few rusty barrels, and some pieces of broken aeroplanes lying around. For half an hour we drove through the desert until Djibouti appeared: clusters of white houses, a few trees. I have a weakness for French colonial cities. Djibouti isn't as romantic as Phnom Penh or Saigon or as grand as Dakar, but it's pleasant enough considering it's one of the hottest places in the world. My room in the sordid Greek hotel had no windows because of the heat, only a hole in the ceiling to let the air in. In the middle of the day the population was not to be seen, presumably they were all lying under punkas or something, digesting the monstrous midday meal the French always insist on eating wherever they are. I wandered round the hot streets, waiting for visiting time to come; for in Djibouti I had a mission. From a friend I had an introduction to a man in Djibouti who knew an old Frenchman who had known the poet Rimbaud who died in 1891. After Rimbaud gave up poetry he lived for eleven years between Djibouti and Harar, living by gun-running and slave-trading. This old man in Djibouti had been employed by Rimbaud as a youth. When I reached his dingy little house there followed a long muddled conversation in fragments of half a dozen languages with a ragged witless Somali who might have been a servant. I was on tenterhooks to see the old man, this surprising piece of history, but no, it turned out finally that he was dead, had been dead for six months. Such is travel. Disappointments like this happen more often than travellers confess. Most of travel is just nothing happening.

It was time to get on the railway. There was a train tomorrow, and I went to the station to buy a ticket. The train situation was that there was a splendid air-conditioned sleeping coach three nights a week to Addis for the use of Europeans and first-class Ethiopians and Somalis; by travelling at night the worst of the heat was avoided. For the second-class Ethiopians, by far the majority of course, there was a train during the day that stopped everywhere; but, said the French official at the station, it was unheard of that a European would travel on this train: the heat, he said, the dirt, the smell, the people. I explained that I wanted to look at the countryside, which would be invisible at night. He looked at me as if I was mad. To travel with the common people, I said, would be of the greatest interest to me; I was studying these people, I continued desperately. I tried the appeal to culture. I was travelling to Harar in the footsteps of Rimbaud, I said, your great French poet. But if he had heard of Rimbaud at all, it must have been the disreputable side, because he got on the telephone to some higher functionary, speaking very rapidly in that special variety of French that it is impossible for foreigners to understand. No, he said, interpreting for me in baby language, it was not permitted for Europeans to travel by the day train, I must go air-conditioned by night.

I gave up, and the following morning solved the problem by simply going to the second-class ticket window and buying a seat from the sleepy Somali clerk. Still I must admit the Frenchman had a point. That train was like a furnace, it was filthy, and the people undoubtedly did smell. They do their hair in a rather special way in Ethiopia, screwing it into numerous tiny plaits, then anointing these with rancid butter and cow dung. The heat brings out the full bouquet of the cow dung, and the butter ran down the black faces of my companions. Otherwise they looked rather splendid, as the Ethiopian national dress is a kind of toga, worn with positively Roman dignity, and under that a kind of riding breeches. Most of the passengers were poor farmers, just travelling from one station to the next. If we were stopped by those armed robbers, there wouldn't be much for them to take. They'd be better advised to wait for the air-conditioned night train. But just in case they got any ideas, we had an armed guard who rode on the roof of the diesel engine. There he slept all day long in the blazing sun, lying uncomfortably on his rifle. The hazards of the Djibouti railway aren't too bad now, but they were once, for this is the district of the fierce Danakil tribe, who used to go in for cannibalism and mutilation. When the railway was being built, a lot of Frenchmen were eaten; nor was even the actual line safe. The Danakil used to steal the rails to melt down and make into spear-heads, and their women used the telegraph wires for bangles and necklaces. Travelling along we saw plenty of Danakil staring at the train, standing in the wilderness in their togas, often standing on one leg like storks. After I had trained myself not to be sick at the smell of the rancid butter, I got on well enough with the other passengers, though we had no word of any language in common. As the passengers mostly changed at each station, I was a continual source of diversion. Little children came to touch my white arms with their dirty black hands. Refreshment was continually offered, consisting always of some curious sour pancakes called injira with the consistency of sponge rubber, and a specially horrible kind of beer called talla, like heavily watered-down stout. Never mind, everyone was very friendly, and delighted that I would consume any of these things.

The next day I continued the Rimbaud trail by native bus from Dire Dawa, the fabulous walled city that Sir Richard Burton had visited a hundred years ago, disguised as an Arab to safeguard his life. For Rimbaud it had been the headquarters of his deplorable business. As we climbed away from the plain, I watched the landscape change. It was cooler, fresher, greener, with that marvellous peppery quality in the air that Burton had noticed. That, and the extraordinary smell of eucalyptus that pervades the atmosphere in the highlands of Ethiopia. Harar is surely one of the few scented cities in the world. I was pleased to see that it looked much as Burton had described and drawn it. The walls are still there, the great mosque, the market—once the greatest in East Africa, the elaborate merchants' houses, the bazaars. In the winding streets of the old town you might be living any time within the last four hundred years. The women of Harar have a great reputation for their beauty, Arab and Somali stock mixed, tall, very dark, smooth-skinned, fine-featured. Burton had remarked on them, and Rimbaud, in very exotic terms, so I was delighted to find they were just my type: tall, long-legged tennis girls that you might see at some Oriental Wimbledon, only wearing muslin dresses embroidered with some Amharic motif, instead of concertina skirts and cardigans.

Naturally it's not a town with a great many diversions: a fleapit cinema, a couple of tatty cafés, one with a billiard table. The chief after-dinner amusement is a slightly macabre one: feeding the hyenas. They gather at the cemetery just outside the walls of the town, and one night my host of the evening drove me to see this feast. It was very dark beneath the walls except for the light from a small brazier where a ragged man sat holding a basin of bones. Where had he got the bones? From the cemetery, of course, said my host: and if we paid him he would call the hyenas to their dinner. We paid him; he called; and there was scuffling in the dark and near the brazier bright points of light appeared in the blackness. The eyes of the hyenas. He called again, with soft native sounds, a name for each separate animal, and they answered to their names, and came to take the bone he tossed into the circle of light round the brazier. One by one they came, growling and whining, and immediately shuffled back into the night where their eyes glowed again. There was a crunching of the bones, and short sharp quarrels between the hyenas. When the bones were gone the dim yellow forms disappeared into the blackness, and the ragged man bent over his brazier again.

It may not sound like it—but Harar is a little paradise in its high bracing mountain valley. It's somewhere one could live quietly for months—eating, writing, walking, sleeping, putting oneself right with the world.

19
Ethiopia : A Schoolboy's Tour of Addis
[January 1962]

THE first thing was the eucalyptus smell. All round the airport there were these clumps of bluish trees, and their scent was in the air, a tangy sort of smell, not romantic at all, really more like part of a cold cure. That was the first of the delicious absurdities of Addis Ababa. The second was the atmosphere, or rather the lack of any. The man who carried my bag was breathing heavily and hoarsely, and I thought poor asthmatic old Ethiopian; but then with the effort of closing the boot of the car the driver was breathing heavily too; and now I began to notice that I was panting myself with doing nothing at all. This was a community where everybody was permanently out of breath. The simple reason: Addis is more than 8,000 feet above sea level and so the air is thin.

We drove towards the city centre, or at least that was the idea, but now another peculiarity of Addis presented itself. It's one of the most primitive cities in the world, and the population is only half a million or so, but I should say Addis sprawls over an area just about the size of Greater London. Outside the airport we passed a cluster of modern houses, then the road plunged into a wood and crossed a mountain stream. We passed an ox-cart and a man in biblical costume riding an ass; then some old women carrying water on their heads in paraffin tins—and now we drove past a huge modern hotel. Blocking our way in the drive was a flock of fat-tailed sheep tended by a shepherd also dressed in biblical clothes. This first taste of

Addis was entirely typical I soon discovered, typical and a bit bewildering.

So was my first encounter with the Amharic language which is what they speak in Ethiopia. In Europe, however little of a language you may know, you can probably work out if it's food or politics that's being discussed, and whether the person speaking is happy or angry. But this was Ethiopia and in the hotel they didn't speak a word of any language I could recognize; nor did it help to see Amharic written, for it resembles nothing so much as the footprints of beetles and the alphabet has got 278 letters.

Without a word of the language I wondered how I was going to find my way around this strange city of eucalyptus groves and roaming sheep; but I had a stroke of luck. I had a lunch appointment this first day, arranged by cable from Cairo. My host was a great Amharic scholar, the wisest man in Ethiopia, so everybody said. Duly he arrived at the hotel, and drove me away to his house through more incongruous scenes. 'That's the University,' he said, pointing at an impressive monumental arch standing at the entrance to a large untilled field. 'They haven't finished it yet. Look at that fellow carrying the sheep round his neck,' and next to him there was a man riding a mule and holding up a white umbrella. A group of lordly-looking fellows wearing spotless white shirts and jodhpurs walked along in the dust in their bare feet. The road was full of holes. Brightly coloured, dilapidated buses racketed past bulging with passengers. What was conspicuous about all the people I saw was their immense dignity and self-possession. They had nothing of the scurrying quality of crowds in Europe. I remembered a pleasing remark I'd read by a Victorian traveller: 'Concerning the Ethiopians their most marked characteristic is their abominable self-satisfaction.' That's the stuff, I thought, they're the boys for me!

But there was still the language problem. Over lunch with the wisest man in Ethiopia the matter was resolved. The food was Ethiopian at my request: a curry with rubbery pancakes called injira, and to drink the fabulous tedj, the Ethiopian champagne. Curry and champagne. Tedj however is really a kind of mead. It's made from honey and it tastes like a rather heady orange juice. My host of course knew where to get the best tedj. The mild orange juice flavour was a delusion, and soon I was babbling recklessly away. I told him about my problem. 'My dear fellow, you must get yourself a schoolboy,' he said. 'You won't get the best out of Addis if you don't. All the schoolboys speak excellent English, and they love to practise it.' This advice was all very well up to a point, all right for sightseeing I supposed (if there were any sights), but I'd heard a lot about the night-life of Addis, and I couldn't take a schoolboy there. However, wait and see.

That afternoon I went along to the New Market, said to be the largest in Africa. Here if I wished I could have bought ostrich eggs, or a Byzantine silver cross, or the stuffed paw of a lion, or a powder horn, or an old-fashioned blunderbuss. Ethiopians are very partial to fire-arms, and a large section of the market was devoted to these, of every possible kind and vintage. Ethiopians tend to be a little formal with each other but this part of the market was noticeably more animated than the rest, with little groups of men fondling each other's weapons, peering down the barrels of revolvers, happily whirling the chambers, no doubt yearning to let them off. In the midst of the Amharic chatter I heard a young voice. 'Englishman?' it said, apparently asking a question, but certain of the answer. I had found my schoolboy. His name was Yasu. He was about fourteen, dressed in grimy khaki pants and incongruous spotless white sandals. His English was fairly good, because his generation are being taught at school entirely in English as part of the Emperor Haile Selassie's plan to bring his primitive country more into the modern world. Young Yasu was no innocent. 'You come and see hangmans,' he said, rather obscurely, and led me along an alley lined with stalls selling ambergris, indigo and other exotic things, to a large empty square dominated by a gibbet; there was no hangman and nobody hanging on the gibbet; but here, a few days earlier, a man had been hanged in public for stealing. This is still the custom in Ethiopia. The excuse is that nothing short of this desperate punishment, conducted in public, will bring home to the ignorant folk of Ethiopia the force of the rule of law. I don't know what had been brought home to Yasu: he described the occasion with some relish and he wished I could have been there to see it.

We passed on through the market, stopping for a lemonade outside a grimy café. A tattered old man offered to clean my shoes; somebody else wanted me to weigh myself on his weighing machine. Yasu suddenly asked: 'Would you like to have an air hostess, a superior air hostess?' I declined, offering the altitude as a particularly inappropriate excuse. He seemed disappointed. Anyway I could see I need have no fears now for the evening.

In the meantime, I thought, what about some more sightseeing. Yasu wasn't very keen, and I could see he wasn't going to be a very informative guide, but at least he could help me to establish my bearings in this strange new city. Yasu fetched a taxi but I said no, a gharry. One might as well go the whole hog, even if this meant losing face with my guide. The gharry was a one-horse affair driven by an almost-naked very black man wearing a sort of deerstalker hat. All over the harness, bells tinkled and jangled as we bounced along the streets among the lordly straight-backed figures in their rags. The driver had a fine whip with a long lash at the end with which he flicked at other gharry drivers. Whenever he saw a lady he knew, which was often, he swept off the deerstalker. From the way the traffic went it was impossible to work out which side of the road they travel on in Ethiopia.

We trotted past the Emperor's palace and I caught a glimpse of the shabby imperial lions in their cages. Alas, the days have gone when he kept a lion chained to each post of his front gate. Only a narrow path in the middle was safe from the reach of either lion. When a man passed through the gate, the lions sprang at him. If he flinched from either and left the narrow central path, he would fall to the claws of the other lion. So cautious a man, the Emperor reasoned, would not be worth having around anyway.

Next I went to look at St. George's Cathedral in the centre of Addis. Here indeed the buildings are a bit closer together, but goats and mules still wander the streets among the modern cars. The Cathedral has some fine frescoes in a Byzantine style, except that alongside the saints the paintings are full of imperial lions and stout Ethiopian warriors with fuzzy hairdos. A nice detail I noticed was that the bad men are always drawn in profile, and only the good men get full-face treatment. All this old stuff was of no interest to my schoolboy who was beginning to get restless, so I gave him his head for the rest of the afternoon.

In turn, we visited a smart hotel, where he had a milkshake; the Metropole Cinema, where they were showing a film called 'The Quite Americaine'; the Sudan Interior Mission, where the lad had been educated; the Ministry of Mapping and Geography, where his cousin worked; and the Zanzi-Bar, where I had a whisky which tasted of petrol.

When we came out it was dark, and in Addis night is really night. Except in the centre, the street-lights are few and feeble. We stumbled along a few streets, with me falling into the craters in the road. Yasu suggested the air hostess again, and I said the altitude again. We turned a corner and there was a strange and delightful sight: a long street of little cabins with open fronts and from every small house shone a red or a green light. The ones with the green lights were bars, the red ones were bars also and something else. We walked along the exciting street, looking in the open doorways. In each house there was a bar, shelves piled with bottles of poisonous drinks and mysterious rows of aluminium kettles; sitting around the bar were girls and a few men, the girls dressed in pretty muslin country costumes like folk-lore singers. The whole feeling was one of innocence and gaiety. If this was seedy then seediness was preferable to respectability. One had the exhilarating feeling of a whole town out on the tiles. We went round a corner and there was another street the same, we went round several more corners, and the red and green houses seemed to be endless. If you looked along the rooftops there was a kind of red glow in every direction. Yasu put me down for an old stick, and he was immensely cheered at my pleasure in all this. 'We go to tedj house,' he said, and we went into a little red house apparently like all the rest, except there were more silver kettles no the shelves and no bottles of poisoned whisky. Glasses were produced and a kettle. Tedj was poured out of the spout. Why tedj is served in this way all over Ethiopia is a complete mystery, profitable anyway to the maker of the kettles. We sat on benches and drank the not very good tedj. On the floor there were skins of wild animals like deer and monkeys; on the walls pictures of Princess Margaret and Mr. Anthony Jones on their wedding day. The girls came and talked to us. I conveyed my compliments through Yasu, but I noticed he was getting a bit abstracted. The girls in their pretty folksy costumes behaved rather like barmaids in an English pub, immensely respectable with that same air of patient self-sacrifice, like nurses in a lunatic asylum.

After a while Yasu said a dollar please, and I gave him one: in Ethiopia it's equivalent to about three shillings. He disappeared through a curtain at the back of the bar, and I sat and waited for him.

The girls smiled at me vaguely, and I smiled at them vaguely; they talked among themselves and I didn't understand; I poured out some more tedj from the tin kettle; outside, the streets glowed the sort of red of children's boiled sweets and music came out of the houses further on. It was my first night in Ethiopia, and I was happy.

20
Ethiopia : Morning in the Piazza
[May 1963]

IN Addis Ababa I always stay in the third best of the three hotels, even when I can afford better. There's a story that it was once the Imperial Brothel; I don't know about that; but anyway these days the guests are innocent enough: people like me, and the belly dancers from the Lebanese night club, and sad-faced men from the Ethiopian provinces, petitioners who have come to Addis to try and get some personal wrong set right at one of the Ministries. They stay in the hotel for months. It's a huge place, built on a curious plan, with a centre block, as it were the brothel administration, and then galleries running along three sides of an open space improbably occupied by a tennis-court. This was rarely used, because Addis Ababa is 8,000 feet up, and that kind of exercise leads straight to a heart attack.

The great thing about the hotel was the quiet. Even on Sunday nights, when the whole town goes on the tiles in Addis, it was quiet there beside the tennis court. Perhaps there would be a brief fracas at four in the morning or so, with the petitioners quarrelling over the belly dancers, but then there'd follow a long deep silence, interrupted for me only when my friend Homer came to pick me up for coffee on his way to the office. This would be about eleven. 'Howdy,' he'd say, in his old-fashioned way, and we'd go round to the Piazza for that coffee.

Homer is an American negro who came to Ethiopia thirty years ago from a little town in Mississippi as the ambassador of a body called the Universal Negro Improvement Association. This longwinded organization had the idea that the black kingdom of Ethiopia, founded these three thousand years, was the ancestral home of the American negro, and the Ethiopians their natural brothers. Homer was the advance guard of a mass migration; until he sent back the news that he was the only negro in the place. He complained that he was hated and despised here to a degree that would be out of the way even in Ole Miss. Thinking him good riddance perhaps, certainly not wishing to throw good money after bad, the Universal Negro Improvers cancelled his return ticket. Eventually Homer came to accept his bitter exile, this Ethiopian humiliation, especially when he realized that it isn't only the negroes that the Ethiopians look down on, but everybody else as well. Among themselves they look down on each other.

The Cosmopolitan was a café in the Piazza, and its terrace was a good place to watch the curious Ethiopian class system. We'd sit there looking at the peasants in from the country for market day. Barefoot and filthy as few other humans anywhere are, they carried themselves in the city as haughtily as ancient Romans. They wore robes that once were white called 'shammas', rather like togas. When addressed by a citizen of Addis, some mere townsfellow, they would draw the hem of this grubby Roman garment across the lower part of their faces, ostentatiously averting their gaze.

The Piazza was the main square of the city, with cars and lorries going by, but everything had to stop while the country gentry crossed in their own time with their sheep and goats. Homer pointed out a great personage wearing a blanket riding on an ass. Dismounting with Old Testament dignity, he tied his donkey to a parking meter. I had been in Addis before, but the parking meters were new. Indeed Ethiopia is making great leaps into the future, and there were all sorts of bizarre novelties in the Piazza. Exuberant twentieth-century inventions like a couple of neon signs and some traffic lights were new too. Amharic, the language of the country, has a curly script that rather lends itself to neon; perhaps that's why the signs are always left on in the daytime. The traffic lights are even more popular. They're regarded purely as a source of entertainment, the traffic bowls by regardless, but there's always a knot of togaed citizens on the corner watching the colours change, greeting the changes with little cries. The commerce in the Piazza is catching up with the times, but there's still plenty of the old Ethiopia. New since last time was a record shop blaring out the Twist all day, Ethiopians inside jogging in St. Vitus time to Mike Sarne, but on the other side of the Piazza there's a bar where a country girl plays the dulcimer.

Guerlain of Paris actually has a branch in the Piazza, where Ethiopian girls with European educations stand by the hour dabbing free-sample scent behind each other's ears, but outside on the pavement peasant women still squat plaiting each other's hair with rancid butter. Across the Piazza is the office of a dealer in musk, the foundation of the most exquisite perfumes. The world's supply comes from Ethiopia, it's milked from wild Ethiopian civet cats, females only, and it smells far worse than rancid butter. Certainly the Piazza was never boring.

'Why's it called the Piazza?' I asked Homer as we drank our coffee. 'Well,' he replied, 'it's in memory of the Italians who murdered all those Ethiopians in the war.' By the same token, he explained, the main street of Asmara (the other big town after Addis) is known to this day as the Viale Mussolini, although it's supposed to be called the Avenue Haile Selassie, after the Emperor. You still see Italians everywhere in Ethiopia, and the Ethiopians love them, because they associate them with war, which they prefer to all other activities. Wretched indeed is the Ethiopian home that hasn't got a little armoury of its own: you know, a few old hand grenades pinched from a British soldier bashed on the head in an alley, or merely a rusty Italian pistol and some clips of cartridges. A cross-country trip in an Ethiopian bus is a special experience, because bandits still flourish outside the towns, and no Ethiopian traveller will go without his carbine. I have seen an old woman carrying a Sten gun. To be allowed to handle another man's weapon is the equivalent of blood brotherhood, and I've proudly had this experience when a friend of mine, Solomon, an Ethiopian prince, prised up the floorboards of his bedroom and brought out his weapons for me to fondle. Even in the Piazza war is always in reach. There's a cinema on the corner that shows nothing but scratchy newsreels of the last war. The soundtrack is relayed through loudspeakers to the streets outside, I suppose in order to tempt passers-by to step in and join the battle, and every night the square echoes to the thunder of the Alamein barrage, the scream of Stukas dive-bombing, the pom-pom-pom of anti-aircraft fire. Thank goodness the Imperial brothel was out of earshot, and during the morning the Piazza is fairly quiet.

Addis rises late. As a non-Ethiopian Homer had to watch his step at the Ministry where he now works, but I don't think he ever got there before half past eleven, and some days he didn't go at all. What he did, I don't know exactly, though it sounded like something to do with public relations. He was always full of information, usually about some desperate hitch in the government's well-meant plans for the betterment of wretched Ethiopia. 'Man,' he'd say, 'd'you hear 'bout the new University. All the money the Parliament vote is spent on the ornamental gates. Fine gates, but no money left to build the University.' This, alas, was true. At the bottom of Churchill Avenue stand these magnificent gates today, giving entrance to an empty field. Again, another morning, Homer—the Jeremiah—leaned confidentially across the coffee table. 'Man, d'you hear 'bout the new dam they build at Koka. All the way from the mountains they bring the building stone. Now they find it's no good, all rotten from the piss of baboons.' When Homer went to work, I'd stay on at the café waiting for Solomon, my princely friend with the guns: we usually lunched together. In the meantime there was the Piazza to pay attention to.

Nobody leaves you alone in Ethiopia, sociability is the delight and the curse of life there, and at the Cosmopolitan you were pestered by little boys selling things round the tables. From a ragged urchin wearing pants made from an old flour sack you could buy lion's claw earrings for your girl or an elephant's hair bracelet to make you brave. Another good buy was the Ethiopian peasant paintings, done with smelly poster colours on crude canvas in a kind of cartoon Byzantine style taken from the murals in the local Coptic churches. Most of them told a story, usually of course something about war, and it was dead easy to distinguish the good people from the bad ones, because the heroes were shown full face, and the villians always in profile. When I asked an Ethiopian friend why, he explained: 'In this way you see the evil-doers but they do not see you, which might be dangerous.' To make sure you don't make any mistake, the evil-doers always have black faces, whereas the good people are given white ones, although of course there are no white Ethiopians. Well, I'd be puzzling over these mysteries, and perhaps feeling the unmistakable signal from within that meant it was time for the first drink of the day, when my friend Solomon would arrive from his office.

Solomon, as I said, is a prince, but the wind of change has blown unkindly to his sort, and he is forced to spend his mornings as an airline clerk. He keeps up his princely ways as best he can, and perhaps it was from some idea of its being an aristocratic sort of drink that he always asked for a gin and tonic. This used to put him back by a good few Ethiopian dollars, because the tonic cost five times as much as the gin. This was Ethiopian economics, due to the fact that everything imported into the country has to come by the Djibouti railway, which is consequently the most expensive in the world. The charges are by bulk, and prices tend to even out rather obligingly in some ways. In Addis caviar (if you could get it) would be cheaper than corned beef, and champagne was about the same price as Empire wine. The only snag was that these obliging prices evened out at a pretty high level. Anyway, Solomon got his gin and tonic and then we went off for our regular Ethiopian lunch.

Long ago I lost whatever enthusiasm I ever had for the national cuisine in outlandish places like this, and indeed the Ethiopians themselves have long since changed to a sensible diet of pizzas and spaghetti, but Solomon is a passionate patriot in all things and will eat nothing but native recipes. Well, it's an interesting but limited diet, and designed for warrior heroes. It certainly gives one, if nothing else, the campaigning feeling. Ethiopian food consists of two dishes, a fierce curry eaten with sour pancakes that smell of damp blankets; and raw meat. Solomon usually had the raw meat, which is reputed to produce the nastiest worms in the world. To have had worms at some time is a kind of condition of manhood in Ethiopia. I once asked a young man if he'd ever had them, and he replied, 'No, Sir, but I hope to soon.' Not hoping to myself, I always had the fiery curry, with its built-in prophylactic. The restaurant where we always went (and where nobody else went, they were having their pizzas and spaghetti) was in a *tukul*, which is the traditional Ethiopian dwelling, actually just a mud hut. We sat on the floor cross-legged on monkey skins, and drank a great amount of tedj, the wine of the country, a delicious kind of mead. It doesn't taste strong, and you drink it out of deceptive slender flasks like little altar lamps that hold more than they appear to. The curry tends to quicken consumption, and before long we were stretched on those monkey skins like emperors at some Lucullan feast. The talk revolved, as it does everywhere, on woman, money, politics and sport.

Solomon is a passionate gamesman: my stock soared when I told him I'd once met Stanley Matthews, and sank to nothing when I didn't know what position on the field he played. Tennis was Solomon's favourite game, and his only memories of a visit to England were watching Wimbledon on television in his hotel in South Kensington. On certain desperate days, after lunch, we would go for coffee to my hotel, the old Imperial brothel with the tennis court, and then there was the danger that Solomon would want to play. Sometimes an opponent could be found, and then I'd take my siesta in the umpire's chair, but once or twice I had to play. It was like that desperate game of billiards in Gilbert and Sullivan, played 'with a crooked cue, on a cloth untrue, and elliptical billiard balls'. The tennis balls were round all right, but the altitude seemed to exaggerate their bounce, so even if one got to the line of the ball (no easy task, after the tedj and curry) the ball would soar like a rocket over one's head. On myself the altitude had an even worse effect. The blood pounded in my ears, a salt taste came in my mouth, and a searing pain in my lungs, and once, briefly but memorably, the sky went black and that was that. Things weren't made any easier by the holes in the net, the absence of lines on the court, and Solomon's temper. Normally a man of courtly courtesy, he became transformed on the tennis court. All the mettlesomeness of his race came to the front. This was the man again who had defended his ancestral home against the Italian soldiers with nothing but a clasp knife. The day the sky went black, Solomon agreed I should be excused from these tennis afternoons. If I became exhausted so easily, he said pityingly, how should I have strength for the evening's drinking with him in the Piazza?

21
Ethiopia : At Mama's Place
[May 1963]

ADDIS ABABA makes an impact like no place else. I remember first driving into the city from the country at night. On the outskirts of Addis the houses are no more than mud huts, but long before the first mud hut I saw a reddish glow in the sky ahead, an alarming, apocalyptic sight, as if the whole place was burning down. Only when I got closer did I realize that this was the red-light district. It's the biggest in the world, and arguably the most innocent. It's literally a red-light district: here in hundreds of tiny bars where the light bulbs are always painted red Ethiopian girls in flowery peasant costume sit waiting to entertain you. Ethiopians are as black as anybody, but more fine featured than most negro people, and a lot of the girls are lovely. It's their job to pour out the drinks. In a few Westernized bars you can get whisky and so on, but talla and tedj are what you have to drink as a rule. Talla is nothing much, ranging, depending on the bar, from a kind of undernourished stout to sheer dishwater; but tedj at its best is a drink to dream of, a dry, faintly sparkling amber liquor made from honey. All over Ethiopia you see hollow gourds hung up in the ever-present thorn trees. The idea is that the bees will build their combs inside the gourd which can then be cut down and the honey fermented. Drinking is something very important to Ethiopians so it's as well the bees co-operate.

And this was how we used to spend every evening in Addis, my friend Solomon and myself. We used to do a tour of several bars, half a dozen or so, and take in different ones every night. There are so many of these places in Addis, and new ones always opening, that you could go through a lifetime's hard drinking in the city without ever visiting the same bar twice. But, wherever we went, we always began the evening at a bar called Mama Tafessa's, for the important reason that my friend Solomon has a passion for tattoos. All the girls in Mama's bar are from the country, some from remote and savage regions, which means something in Ethiopia, and their complexions are weirdly and wonderfully stitched and embroidered. Solomon would sit beside me in the lurid gloom cast by the one naked red-painted electric bulb and play at spotting the tribes. Cupping his little flask of amber wine, he'd point to a pretty girl with a bluish barbed-wire pattern across the bridge of her nose. 'She's from Tigre,' he'd say, and I'd be impressed, because the Tigrinya are savage and uncontrollable even by Ethiopian standards. 'That's a Gambela girl,' Solomon would say, pointing out a terrifying tattoo consisting of crocodile-teeth markings all round her mouth. 'They make good wives,' he added. But his favourite was a hefty girl from some remote tribe on the Sudan border who had an extraordinary bicycle chain motif round the line of her chin stretching from ear to ear like a grin. 'Mama says this girl is very passionate,' Solomon said, and there was something about her that appealed even to my etiolated Northern soul.

Mama herself was the dominant personality. She was a huge, dirty woman from Harar in the Eastern part of the country. Her age was strictly undefinable, as is the case with these women when they're no longer young. She might have been thirty-five or seventy-five. Solomon had no time for Mama, but I liked her tattoo better than any. In the centre of her forehead she wore a tattoo exactly like that cabbalistic sign you see on the front cover of any book of Somerset Maugham. I refrained from sending Mr. Maugham a postcard, but I did mention him one night to Mama. No connection, she said, briskly. All the same the cultural level at Mama's place was high. She was especially proud of the pictures on her wall, which were those desolate coloured views of Alpine valleys, sunshine at Sorrento, fishermen at Ibiza, and so on, that the travel agencies put out. Pride of place was occupied by a huge picture torn out of a magazine of Princess Margaret and Lord Snowdon. Every bar in Addis has one of these, the only person more popular in Ethiopia is Sophia Loren, but at Mama's the royal couple were in colour and framed, and on a shelf beneath sometimes burned a small candle, as if at a shrine. Music goes on ceaselessly in all these bars, usually just the radio blaring out Italian tunes, but Mama is proud of her long-player and she's got a pile of twist discs. Mama's general up-to-dateness and high cultural tone are accentuated by her European clothes, usually a tubular tweed skirt, not at all clean, and a stained blouse fastened with a chipped brooch. In spite of her outlandish appearance, she is always elaborately polite, even to Solomon, because after all he is a Prince.

Princes are thick on the ground in Ethiopia, there's not much usually to distinguish them from anybody else, but Solomon gives full value. To look at, he's like one of those little illustrations in the margins of dictionaries, depicting the word Prince: everything combines, the haughty gaze from piercing wide-set eyes; his nose curved and sharp as a scimitar; the nostrils flared like a thoroughbred; a supercilious thin smile; an over-riding air of pitying condescension. I'm awfully fond of him, but I must admit, to meet, he can be a bit disconcerting. You must be prepared to play second fiddle. Like all Ethiopians, Solomon has a low opinion of all non-Ethiopians, and though he is, I think, fond of me, he cannot understand why I am not an Ethiopian. When drunk, which he always is by midnight, he believes that I am one, and he gossips about the relatives which he thinks we have in common and he talks in Amharic of which I don't understand a word. I didn't mind. It's quite common, after all, for communication to break down as the evening advances. Until then, Solomon was always patient, answering my endless tourist's questions carefully, though asking few in return. He didn't ever want to leave Ethiopia, and he didn't care about what went on in other and inferior places. Mama, on the other hand, was always on at me for news of the outside world. How was Sophia Loren? What was this about her being a bigamist? How was Churchill getting on? Or she'd draw her elephant's foot stool closer for a question she didn't want the girls to hear. This changing a man into a woman: what exactly did they *do*? Solomon disapproved of Mama's curiosity. To him sex-change was a non-Ethiopian matter and so of no possible interest. When Mama was on with her questions, Solomon would beckon to the girl with the bicycle chain tattoo, and she'd come over and sit beside him. With a loving finger he would trace that wonderful tattoo.

While Mama was plying the tedj kettle round, I'd take a look at the other customers. Usually there were not more than half a dozen or so, for the bar was small, and they were often students from the University. Work is unpopular in Ethiopia, and students tend to stay students for as long as they can. Here they were stoking up for the Twist. The Ethiopians are rather like the English in several ways. They're snobby and rather pleased with themselves, and they're also, as C. E. Montague observed of the English, permanently half a dozen drinks below par. At Mama's tremendous silences reigned while the leeway was made up. Solomon would stare arrogantly at the opposite wall, the students at the floor, the girls in the corner whispered and tittered. The tedj flasks were filled and emptied, increasingly fast, until eventually break-through point was reached, and Mama brought Chubby Checker out of his tattered sleeve. The long-player was started, and soon everybody was twisting, the empty kettles were bouncing on the bar, and more people would begin to come in from the street, attracted by the music. Ethiopians are as stuffy as we are, but now it was possible to speak to strangers without being introduced. As always, this had its risks. The affable stranger easily becomes the night-long bore. At Mama's place there was an extra hazard. One of her cultural amenities was the high class seating. She had bought up some chairs from a bankrupt cinema: they had tip-up seats and were joined indivisibly in pairs, with a common armrest. You had to be careful who you invited to sit next to you. Once a determined man was settled in the tandem seat, you had him for the night.

Bores can be boring on any subject, but the worst the English traveller can face abroad is the language bore, that terrible friendly single-minded self-improver on the scrounge for a free English lesson. I've had my fill of them, so it was insane of me one evening, seeing a shy young man with a book, to ask him over for a penn'orth of tedj. It was the book that interested me: here, I reasoned foolishly, was an Ethiopian intellectual, a man to tell me all the answers to put in the articles about the Ethiopian political scene, that uniquely confused subject, which I couldn't get round to writing.

'Er, tell me,' I said to begin, 'what are you reading?' He handed me the book and I knew the worst. It was *'Oliver Twist* by Charles Dickens; abridged by J. C. McPhail, Bachelor of Commerce, Aberdeen, author of *David Copperfield, Henry IV, Part II, Pride and*

Prejudice, etc., etc.' I spared a thought for J. C. McPhail in his bed-sitter in Grub Street, blue pencil in hand, bent over—what would it be now?—*Far From the Madding Crowd*, *The Mill on the Floss*, *Tom Jones*. He'd brought down *Oliver Twist* to eighty pages. Throughout I found the young man had underlined the difficult words, pending translation by some generous English speaker like myself. On page one, words like *porridge*. Hurriedly I gave the book back. 'Why do you want to learn English?' I said to the young man. I needn't have worried about his being shy. In a voice vibrant with Ethiopian self-importance, he replied: 'I wish to be a business man.' In the next pair of seats I saw Solomon pull a face. Business is a sore point with the Ethiopian nobility. Traditionally they are landowners who do not stoop to commerce, and as a result all the money in Ethiopia is made by Italian or Lebanese middlemen. Lately the wind of change has been blowing unkindly, and Solomon is forced to spend his days as an airline clerk. It is a situation he can't forgive.

'Why do you want to be a business man?' I tediously asked the young man. 'Because business is the chief cause of civilization.' 'What's that?' said Solomon, with a face like thunder. 'Business men have made every great nation,' the young man replied sententiously. He turned to Solomon. 'Admit to me, sir, there are no business men among monkeys. They are nothing but chatterers. Do not be a chatterer, sir. Nothing can be done by talk.' In another age Solomon would have had his head. Instead he stood up abruptly, and his seat flipped back with a bang. He said goodnight stiffly to Mama, threw me a commanding glance, and went to the door. Rather abjectly I followed him, turning to say goodnight to the young man. He was gazing at the wall, looking at the picture of Lord Snowdon with the candle burning at the shrine. 'Tell me,' the young man said, 'is he a good king?' A vast despair came over me. How could I ever explain? I fled behind Solomon into the street outside. We stumbled along the rutted lanes between the tedj houses. From each house came a red glow, and sounds of music and laughter. We wandered along the lanes, and wherever we turned there were these red chinks in the darkness, and the music. Suddenly I felt wildly happy. Solomon looked at me and, relenting, smiled. 'Well, where shall we go now?' he said.

22

South West Africa : Skeleton Coast
[April 1964]

I WOKE lying on the beach under the wing of the plane. It was just before dawn and still too early for the fog, but out of my sleeping bag it was bitter cold. This was latitude twenty, just inside the Tropic of Capricorn, but the big Atlantic rollers I could see storming in down the beach came from the icy Benguela current, straight from the Antarctic, sweeping up the desert coast of South West Africa. I jumped up and down in the sand to warm up; then stared out at the grey sea; at the little yellow plane on the beach above the high-water flotsam, with my friend Jan lying curled up under the wing of his sand-hole; and then away up the beach at the row of huge dunes advancing into the mist, the beginning of the desert that goes inland for a hundred miles here.

This was Skeleton Coast, the barren strip where the Namib desert of South Africa meets the Atlantic, where for a thousand miles from the Angola border to the Cape Province there's nothing but driftwood and wrecks and the lonely graves of sailors and prospectors. Sailors who've died of thirst, because to be cast ashore on Skeleton Coast is to exchange for the cold sea a place even less hospitable; and prospectors because this is diamond country. My friend Jan is a diamond man, among other things, and yesterday we'd flown up the coast in the little Cub to look up a prospecting pal of his. This was last autumn when they were having one of their periodical, usually fruitless, diamond rushes in South West, and we flew for hours over the claims pegged out in the desert, each a little iron plate like a tombstone marking the funeral of some prospector's hopes. We never saw anybody actually mining, and we couldn't find Jan's friend, though we came down once to ask the way. The coast goes on interminably, steep dunes dropping into the sea like cliffs, and no sign that man ever came here, but suddenly in the sand beneath was a tiny corrugated-iron hut and a clutter of rusting mining machinery. We landed on a bumpy strip by the sea, marked only by the bleached white ribs of a stranded whale, each as tall as a man. The wind howled among the dunes and the place seemed deserted, but then a little old man came out of the hut, with a white beard, and a crushed hat and very dirty. He wasn't pleased to see us; he didn't know where our friend's camp was, and looked as if he wouldn't tell us if he did. He just stood there in the dusty wind, with his hands on his hips and waited for us to go away. suspicious because, as Jan explained, pirates aren't unknown on Skeleton Coast. A plane from Angola with a couple of men drops in at a lonely diggings where the prospector has been massing diamonds for a month or two; and the next thing is the man is found, perhaps months later, with a hole in his head and his diamonds gone.

Now it was getting late, we'd flown too far to get home to Jan's farm in daylight, so he put the Cub down on a friendly stretch of hard beach and we made a fire. It had been a literally fabulous day in this land of wonders. Before breakfast we'd driven from the farm to walk through a petrified forest of trees turned to stone a hundred million years ago. In the solid rock the delicate rings of the growing wood were preserved in perfection. Walking back to the car we crossed a dried up river-bed where I stood in the footprints of a dinosaur. South West Africa is probably the oldest land in the world.

Then we flew down to Cape Cross, the dreary sand pit where five hundred years ago the Portuguese navigator Diego Cam first set foot in Southern Africa. He left a stone cross, and today a replica stands on the margin of the desert and the sea. At Cape Cross we found the guano tables and a seal colony. The economy of South West Africa is a simple one, based largely on picking up things that are there, such as the diamonds and the guano, which is the droppings of sea birds and makes magnificent fertilizer. To search around for this stuff would be a trouble, so the guano farmers have put up enormous tables on the beach, like huge ping-pong tables; and the birds are very obliging and use them; so all the guano farmer has to do is come round once a year with a shovel. It's surely the easiest way of making money ever thought of.

We came in low over the tables and were down to twenty feet at the seal colony. Twenty feet at 150 miles an hour is exciting. This is one of the biggest concentrations of seals in the world, and the beach was black with thousands of them, lolling in their herds, reaching up their beautiful sleek heads to bark at the plane as we roared over. The only Skeleton Coast entertainment not available was the extraordinary sulphur islands, islands that at some times of the year rise up out of the sea just offshore and belch green and yellow flames and then sink back again.

So we flew away up the coast to look for Jan's prospecting friend, to meet the unfriendly little grizzled man, and to sleep on the beach. Now, the next morning, the sun showed at last above the dunes and it was time to be off, still on the diamond trail. On Skeleton Coast the desert gets very hot under the sun, but the sea stays cold, the hot wind from the desert meets the cold and makes fog and already at breakfast time a white mist was swirling along the beach. But on Skeleton Coast there is nothing you can hit in to, so we flew straight off into the whiteness. We were going to Oranjemund for lunch, some five hundred miles down the coast on the South African border where there's the richest diamond mine in the world. In a way it's not really a mine, because here too the diamonds can be more or less picked up, at least they're never more than a few feet deep and they're all in a narrow strip along the edge of the sea where they've been washed in by the waves over many centuries. This means that they're fairly easy to find, and more important, fairly easy for *anyone* to find; and that's the cause of the extraordinary phenomenon called Oranjemund.

For a hundred miles north of Oranjemund Skeleton Coast has another name, the Sperregebiet, Afrikaans for the Forbidden Place. This is where the diamonds are, and nobody may enter the Sperregebiet without permission. Even Jan, though absolutely trusted and anyway too rich already to be tempted, had to make a detour sixty miles inland where the forbidden territory extends, and from the plane once we saw the diamond patrol, two Land Rovers making their way through the dunes, policing the desert where there are no roads or water, but where occasionally desperate men with stolen diamonds try to make their way.

At Oranjemund we were met at the airstrip and taken straight in a car to the X-ray Centre. Coming in and going out, no man visits Oranjemund, not even Oppenheimer himself, the multi-millionaire head of the Diamond Corporation, without being X-rayed from top to toe. A diamond sounds an easy thing to smuggle, being so valuable for its size, but on an X-ray it shows up like almost nothing else, and the sharp eye of the young Irishman in the white coat who operates the image intensifier at Oranjemund (as this safe kind of X-ray is called) wouldn't fail to spot it. (He spotted the threepenny bit I'd craftily hidden in my mouth.) Nor is there any other way to get a diamond out of the Sperregebiet; the desert is impossible, the sea full of dangerous currents and sharks. Indeed, the place sounds like a prison, a kind of Devil's Island on land, but the seven thousand people who live there don't seem to mind it. Over lunch they explained the regime to us: it sounded like one of those Brave New 1984 Worlds.

Everybody in Oranjemund works for the Company, and the Company does everything for you. Everything is provided; your house, furniture, your light and fuel, servants, schools, hospitals, shops. You don't even have to pay your bills, because the Company just deducts them from your salary. After work, the Company looks after your leisure. There's a cinema, a church, a sports club, just one of each, so you won't be put to the trouble of choosing. Indeed the theme of this diamond paradise is a sort of compulsory togetherness. Lunch was like a meal at boarding school or in the Army. The General Manager entertaining us talked about 'civilians' (meaning visitors like us), and 'privileges' (that the inmates got), and 'the camp spirit', though to my mind the camp spirit was rather spoiled by what he told us of the Company's policy of encouraging informers. If you suspect your mate of salting away a diamond, you'll get paid nicely for letting the Company know. 'After all,' the General Manager said, 'diamonds *are* the object of the operation.' 'I must say I don't see why you don't all go balmy,' I said. 'Well,' he said, 'there was a rather nasty murder last year, and a couple of suicides, but most people settle down pretty well'. What about drink? 'Oh, well, you know there's only one bar at the club, and we try and keep a friendly eye at any rate on the new chaps, the ones on their first contract.' Does anybody ever come back for a second contract? 'Oh, yes,' the Manager said, 'they usually come back. You might get a few giving it a try on the outside, but after a spell in the camp they tend to find the going out there pretty tough. After all we do everything for them here.'

After lunch we were driven around the Camp, the long straight streets of identical houses with arc lamps that are left on all night, the shopping centre and the interdenominational church, the hydroponics farm where they grow their vegetables from chemicals; and then we went to see the magic of mining for diamonds, which is really a matter of sorting stones. Of the wonders of South West Africa, this place seemed almost the weirdest, as we exposed ourselves once again to the Irishman in the white coat and his clever machine. 'I'll give you a tip,' he said afterwards, when it was too late. 'Next time hide the diamond in a hollow tooth. It comes up on the X-ray just like a filling. Or better, put it in a baby. We don't X-ray babies.'

And with that piece of useless advice, which however *you* might file away for use some time, we flew off from Oranjemund, back for dinner to Jan's farm in the great grazing lands behind the desert strip, a vast affair of no less than fifty thousand acres where he farms the Karakul sheep from whose pelts so-called Persian lamb furs are made. My friend lives in an extraordinary house at the hub of this huge farm, a kind of human equivalent of the natural wonders of South West. It's called Schloss Duwisib, and it's a German schloss, complete with turrets, arrow slits, oak panelling and stone-flagged baronial hall, set down at first sight unaccountably in the African wilderness. It wasn't built by my sane friend Jan: his father had taken it over when he bought the farm, from the estate of a German baron who was killed in the first World War. He had built the castle in the days fifty years ago when South West was a German colony.

As we sat at dinner at Schloss Duwisib I heard about this strange man, Oberleutnant Baron Hansheinrich Von Wolf, a German nobleman who'd made his career in the German Colonial Army. Made it and broken it, because as well as being obviously a flamboyant and resourceful man the Baron was also a coward, and faced on one occasion with a mob of naked Hottentots armed only with spears, he'd abandoned a battery of field guns and ordered his men to run for their lives. That would have been the end of the Baron in Prussian South West, but for his wife, a legendary figure still in the territory, blonde and beautiful, an American heiress with a will stronger than the Baron's and an understanding of human nature derived from the great Sigmund Freud, one of whose first disciples she was. Her name was Jetta, and Jetta knew a cure for a set-back like the Baron's. His ego must be bolstered, he must be supplied indeed with a sort of artificial super-ego which would cow the insolent burgers who were laughing at his disgrace. Providentially inheriting a fortune from her father just at the right time (he was a manufacturer of quack medicines in Philadelphia), Jetta conceived the idea, Freudianly enough, of building a castle on the precise site of the Baron's disgrace. Now Duwisib is the Hottentot for 'the place without water'—not the most obvious site for a replica of a Rhine castle, but Jetta was not deterred. Here in his oak-panelled hall the Baron would entertain the cream of the colony. Governors and Commissioners would ride a hundred miles to sit at his table. Bygones would be bygones, musicians would play Strauss in the gallery, and the drinking songs would sound out over the great farm while the Niersteiner and champagne flowed until dawn.

The Baroness laid out her fortune: carpets came from Persia, china from China, a chef from Paris; and her cure, I'm happy to report, was a total success. The Baron was welcome again in good society, invitations to the castle were on all the best mantelpieces in South West, he was even elected to the Colonial Legislature.

Even his end, my friend told me, as we sat drinking Niersteiner, too, under the Baron's chandeliers, must have pleased his benefactor Freud. When the First War began, and the British occupied South West, the Baron passed through the enemy lines dressed as a woman and somehow made his way to Europe. There, in the service of the Kaiser, an Oberleutnant once more, he died on the fields of Flanders; far enough away from the turret of his castle in Africa where we climbed after dinner, to sit on the ramparts and talk about him, while the moon rose over the bare hills, looking as old as the ancient and fabulous land beneath us.

23
Egypt : The Black Museum
[June 1964]

THESE days we're all travellers, but some places are nicer than others, and for me the further away the better. Palma or Capri you can keep; Athens or Beirut might be better; but for me the great world really begins where the Mediterranean ends, at Port Said, a place I have a special affection for, shared I wouldn't be surprised by practically nobody else. I used to have a job in Cairo, and Port Said was where we went for week-ends. Those were the days of the Pashas and European influence in Egypt—plenty of kowtowing as we sat with tea and scones in the shambling gardens of the Palace Hotel or strolled along the breakwater to the statue of Ferdinand de Lesseps standing sentry at the entrance to the great Canal that he built. There was a little bar with chairs outside where we'd sit with warm frothy beer and watch the ships go by.

It was seven years before I was in Port Said again, stopping for a few hours off a ship to the East. It was October 1956 and two days before the Suez landings. It was the Egypt now of Nasser instead of Farouk, but nothing much had changed. De Lesseps was still on guard at the Canal entrance, the beer was still warm in the little bar on the breakwater, and for all the new Egypt the bazaar sharks still clamoured with their bad bargains. We put Port Said behind, and afterwards, safely through the Canal and steaming down the Red Sea, we read in the tatty ship's newspaper of the bombardment of the little town by French and British forces. In the days that followed that smudgy, cyclostyled sheet with the purser's

Egypt: The Black Museum

misspellings seemed somehow the appropriate place to read about what we've come to call the Suez Adventure, that imperialist swansong.

I didn't see Port Said again until last year. After another seven years I was looking forward to the sleepy place with its exciting harbour, and of course I was curious to see what legacy Suez had left. I was on deck early as we waited among the other ships in the bay for our turn to enter the Canal. There was the town with its familiar ochre-coloured buildings in all the styles of East and West, with the lines of washing on the roofs and the Egyptian kites circling above; and the only difference seemed a few nasty gaps near the foreshore where French and British shells had fallen, and (oh alas!) another gap, or rather a mere stump, where de Lesseps' statue had stood, smashed now by the Egyptians in revenge.

Soon we were ashore and the little bar was still there, I was happy to see, with the rocky tin tables and the flies floating in the warm beer. Comfortingly, the bazaar sharks were there still too, important-looking men with fly-whisks, hovering about; and I waved them away. I stationed myself to watch the world go by, and bought a paper, learning with no surprise from the Nasserite editorial that we British were imperialistic jackals who gave comfort to the enemies of Arab unity. When my beer came, the waiter who brought it surprisingly sat down at the table. He was a young man in a cowboy shirt with the genuinely friendly smile that Egyptians always have for strangers. He hadn't shaved lately and in one eye he wore the tragic blue spot of trachoma. He explained in a confidential way that he wasn't selling anything; he was a guide. If there were anything to see in Port Said I would surely have seen it already, so I said I didn't need a guide, but he replied, 'You like to see the Black Museum. Very good, very new; Black Museum, very good; Black Museum...' and eventually, weakly, I said why not. Anyway it was an excuse to go wandering through the streets with somebody to translate and to tell me what was going on. To do nothing is one of the great pleasures in Egypt, and that's what everybody in Port Said was doing, strolling in the shady streets, squatting on the ground, leaning against walls. My guide seemed to know everybody in town, and as he discussed me with his friends I hoped he wasn't saying that here was another imperialist jackal who'd given comfort to the enemies of Arab unity. There was a mocking note in their laughter, and thinking of Suez, I had some idea of what the Black Museum might be.

Round a shabby corner, we came to a square, all shining bright and modern. The new buildings round the square were schools and clinics, my guide explained, that had risen since 1956 out of the ruins of the worst of the Suez bombardment. In the middle of the square was a high, grey, imperious-looking plinth, a monument apparently to the Suez dead; and the plinth stood above a squat and grim sort of mausoleum that reminded me of the one in Red Square in Moscow where Lenin lies alone. This apparently was the Black Museum. My guide in the cowboy shirt led me across a lawn where children were playing, and we went down some steps to a heavy iron door that had a final sort of look. Inside was a large square room, rather dark and quite empty, except for paintings and placards hanging round the walls. The guide took me straight to the paintings, with what I interpreted as a proud smile. They were miserable, crude things that would have been an embarrassment to a church bazaar, but they showed scenes that you would never see there. It was the Suez Adventure. In one picture an Egyptian corpse lay with limbs severed while women in black shawls mourned. In another a British paratrooper falling from the sky was being set upon by citizens armed with what looked like kitchen choppers. In yet another a paratrooper drove his bayonet through the body of an Egyptian child. The paratroopers were drawn with the brush of hatred. They had the faces of foxes, and when they walked they crouched like apes.

In some way the crude exaggeration of these paintings only increased their power. One primitive sketch showed half a man, cut off at his chest, so that he could not be alive; yet, impossibly, his dark eyes were imploring a British soldier for mercy. The painting was done as if by a child who has seen more than a child should. Sometimes the tragedy of this strange art tilted over into cruel farce. On one wall a wretchedly vulgar quilted cushion-cover portrayed an atrocity, and a pokerwork cartoon of the Cosy Corner type bore instead of some facetious slogan the words: The Memory of Our Martyrs Will Live Forever.

That wasn't all on the walls. There were clippings of newspaper headlines about Suez, already yellowing; posters; press photographs. In Accra an angry mob was burning a British car; in Moscow and in

Egypt: The Black Museum

Peking they were marching, under banners accusing Eden. There was Krushchev scowling, and Mao Tse Tung looking impassive. In Trafalgar Square crowds were listening to a dim figure that looked like Bertrand Russell, and the banners were flying here too: LAW NOT WAR, they said, and EDEN MUST GO. Looking at these relics in this strange cellar in Port Said, it all seemed a long time ago. There was an illuminated scroll in Chinese, doubtless pledging the support of the Chinese People's Republic. As for the Egyptians themselves, right across one wall was written in huge capitals OUR CANAL and underneath were elaborate maps and diagrams demonstrating in the style of propaganda for Jehovah's Witnesses or the Flat Earthers, that the Suez Canal was really built by the Egyptians hundreds of years before de Lesseps was heard of. In an alcove to one side I noticed a cinema screen with a huddle of chairs in front of it. My guide had been watching me anxiously for signs of appreciation and, perhaps, contrition. Pointing at the little cinema, I asked him, to be polite, what they showed there. 'Films of War,' he replied. I looked around for something in this chamber of horrors that I could praise with a good conscience. I noticed a rather pretty water-colour, that might have been done by a talented child, showing parachutists floating dreamily down a moonlit sky. 'I like that,' I said to please him.

'You *like*?' he replied eagerly, and I realized in the friendly phrase, but too late, that he thought I *wanted* the thing. Oh God! I hadn't lived in Egypt once not to learn how inconvenient Egyptian obligingness can be. With a happy smile my young man began to tear the painting off its backing. The museum wasn't empty either of visitors or attendants, and alarm bells began to ring in my head. The exhibition had been a bit depressing, but this was positively dangerous. I knew my Egyptian police from old. I knew what happened to anyone unfortunate enough to be caught in the toils of that tortuous bureaucracy. And I couldn't blame them. Here was I, an imperialist jackal if ever there was one, about to be caught robbing a national shrine, caught red-handed with the evidence. I would go to prison, and my boat would sail without me. I grabbed at my guide, and half the picture came away in his hand. He held out the prize to me with a proud smile, and I stuffed the paper in my pocket, concealing the evidence, and made for the door.

Outside in the sunshine I walked rapidly away, but nobody seemed to be following except the cowboy shirt. I told the wretched youth to go away, but he only smiled wider. 'Now we are friends,' he said, actually meaning friends, not merely accomplices. 'My name is Abdul,' he said. 'You like to come and meet my brother?'

Abdul's brother had a shoe-shine shop in one of the little shabby streets we had come along. I was introduced, and seated on a bench with the other customers. From the wall a portrait of Nasser in his most imperious mood inspected me critically, and the radio yelled what sounded like death to all imperialist jackals, but everybody in the shoe-shine shop wanted to shake hands. Somebody passed me a visiting card, and an elderly man in a fez asked me to teach him English. Abdul brought me a fizzy drink that was warm and tasted of boiled sweets. With difficulty I restrained his brother from giving a free shine to my suede shoes. Children in the street stopped to grin through the open door at the white-faced foreigner.

I asked the brothers to lunch, and we went down to the beach, to a restaurant with rough tables on the sand, under a canopy of palm leaves. Here we ate all the delicious Egyptian things I remembered, tahina and kous-kous and a splendid kebab, and drank zebib and beer, and watched the ships coming into the canal, their funnels jutting above the houses. Inevitably we talked of Suez and Abdul gave an interesting account of the landings seven years before. The British, he said, had not behaved well, he was sorry to say. They had dressed up in Russian uniforms and painted Russian flags on their tanks and armoured cars. The Egyptians, misled in this wicked way into expecting friends, had been caught off their guard. Though when the deception was discovered, of course, they rallied and drove the British into the sea. Farcical as this version of events was, I had to admit to myself that it wasn't much more unbelievable than a lot of the tales we'd been asked to believe at the time. Still, there'll always be an England, and the British Lion rallied in my unworthy breast, and I told Abdul he was talking a load of rubbish. He was surprised, he was pained, he turned to his brother: Why, had they not seen the tanks and heard the Russian soldiers speaking English? The brother nodded, and then said something in Arabic. Abdul's face cleared and he patted my hand understandingly. 'Of course,' he said, 'in your country is very much propaganda. They are speaking lies to mistake the people.' He gave me a sweet smile. 'Never mind. Today here we are friends,' and he searched through the bus tickets and unpaid bills in his breast pocket and produced that eternal talisman of friendship, a snapshot of his children. Other snapshots followed: Abdul in his army uniform, Abdul in his flowered shirt, Abdul with an American sailor, holding hands. On these important international occasions I always have a strong card to play: a melting photograph of my small and very blond son. The brothers bent over him with cries of admiration. Then we exchanged addresses, and Abdul said he would come to London very soon and I said I would come back to Egypt and give him lessons to improve his of course already excellent English. The brother said I could stay with his family any time I liked in their room above the shoe-shine parlour. We drank some more beer, and lay on the beach in the sun until it was nearly time for the ship. They they walked all the way back to the quayside with me, and the brother slipped into somebody's garden on the way and stole a huge pink magnolia which he presented to me with a bow. Back on the ship after the farewells I realised guiltily that I had quite forgotten to give Abdul his guide's fee, and he had forgotten to ask for it.

Looking in my pocket for his address, I found a piece of crumpled paper with bright colours on it: part of a watercolour in a child's style, showing parachutists floating dreamily down out of a moonlit sky.

24
Ghana : I Fell into a Storm Drain
[July 1961]

ONE night recently I was walking along in Accra, down in the market part of the town, sober and alert, when I fell into the storm drain. It wasn't what we think of as a drain here. These drains in West Africa are to cope with the terrific rainstorms they have, and they are open drains about five feet deep and almost too wide to step across (they have little bridges). So there was some excuse that, staring at the exciting strangeness of the Accra streets and not looking where I was going, I should fall into this drain—which was full of what you'd expect to find in a drain. I was wet to the waist, and my spectacles fell off. When I found them, groping about, I climbed out, feeling rather shocked and with a cut thumb. What I needed was a *wash*. And also a beer, I thought.

Nobody seemed to have seen me fall, or heard the splash. There are no street lights in this part of Accra, and in the dark I could see scattered shops and houses where a naked electric bulb burned. I went over to one of these. 'I wonder, do you mind, can you tell me where I can find somewhere to have a wash?' I said. It was a shop selling tinned things and the Ghanaian in charge immediately abandoned his customers, two fat black mammies, and disappeared into the back of the shop behind some sacking. The mammies stared at me, and giggled; it wasn't usual to find a white man down this end of the town, especially one so dirty, wet, and malodorous as I was. After a minute the shopman came back with another Ghanaian dressed in the marvellous toga-like robes they often wear, and also, thank goodness, with an enamel basin of water and a piece of soap. Tins of sardines and condensed milk were shovelled aside to make room for my wash. Some fiery iodine was produced for my sore thumb. I was feeling much better now, and full of thanks for all this kindness—so much the normal thing in Africa—but it was my host who was apologising. He wanted to take me for a beer but—'the shop', he said, rolling his eyeballs round the wobbling stacks of tins. But his *friend* . . . And at this the man in the toga smiled as if at some immense compliment. His friend was a policeman well known in Accra (I wondered for what); he was off-duty today, that's why he was wearing his national costume, not his uniform, and *he* would be delighted to drink beer with me. So, after much hand-shaking and clapping on the back, off I went with the friend.

Then I had an idea. As I say, I was feeling fine now, except for my rather clammy trousers. Did the policeman mind if we didn't have a beer, but couldn't we get some palm-wine instead? After all, I remembered, to drink palm-wine was one of the reasons why I'd come to West Africa. My idea went down fine with the policeman. Putting his arm through mine he said his name was Kofi, and we would go at once to a palm-wine bar he knew. He laughed with delight at the idea. An Englishman drinking palm-wine! He was a huge man, and he laughed like thunder. I could see I was in for a good evening.

What did I do, Kofi asked me as we went along—what was my work? I told him I was a journalist. Was I married? Yes, I was. Any children? Yes. How many? Boys or girls? Did I have a picture? In fact I had, of my small son, and this was what cemented our friendship. A family man *and* a drinker—like himself! We arrived at the palm-wine bar which turned out to be a little tented enclosure in the street open to the sky, rather like a temporary lavatory at a country gymkhana. Inside were two long benches with a crude low table in between. On the table were some calabashes filled with a liquid that looked like ginger beer. Palm wine. My friend Kofi knew everybody, in a way that everyone in Africa seems to know everyone else, indeed seem to be related to them, and perhaps are. I was introduced all round, and everyone expressed more wonder at an Englishman wanting to drink palm-wine. They were a shaggy lot, and very nice. Half-a-dozen hands stretched towards me with bowls of palm-wine, but Kofi intervened. He rose and beckoned me to follow him. This I didn't want to do, I wanted my first taste of the palm-wine that I'd come all these thousands of miles for, but he practically dragged me out. 'Look!' he said outside the tent, 'look, I told these fellows you are working with me.' 'In the Police?' I said. 'Yes,' he went on, 'I said you were before here, when the British were in Ghana. You were police chief then. Now you come back to Accra on secret mission. You ask for me, old friend. You are secret service man working with me.' 'But why?' I asked. 'Better for me,' said Kofi. 'Journalist no good. Secret service man English friend very good.' 'All right,' I said. It was all the same to me and anyway I rather fancied myself in the part. We went back into the tent, Kofi and his cloak-and-dagger friend. Palm-wine was a great success.

It tastes, as you might expect, rather like coconut water, though in fact it comes from the palm-tree, which they tap, and not from the nut. It's slightly fizzy and has the flavour of a nursery drink, but I could see by the state of one or two of my new friends that it was something more. Indeed after half-an-hour and a couple of large calabashes, I was feeling quite ready to talk about my secret service work. However, I felt perhaps that it wasn't quite the right thing to bring it up myself, and with a fine sense of security the Ghanaians were not mentioning it. Instead we talked about my small boy, whose picture was passed round, and about this and that. Suddenly the crowd on the opposite bench parted with surprising formality to make room for a newcomer, a rather ugly little man with the gloomiest face I have ever seen. He seemed to be a friend of Kofi's. We went on drinking, and gradually the crowd thinned out, perhaps because the gloomy man had come, I thought. By now my trousers had dried into a kind of volcanic crust. Soon there was only the three of us left; then Kofi leant forward to me. 'Joe says (that was the gloomy man) will you do him great honour to come to his mother's funeral. Yesterday she die, tomorrow she bury. Tonight is big party.' It seemed I was being invited to a wake of some sort, and of course I wanted to go. Kofi said: 'Please you will go as Joe's friend, you shake hands with the father, son, daughter, with the relatives, you say sorry mother die.' I began to feel I was putting my nose in where I wasn't wanted, but after all it was Joe asking me; so I said Yes thank you very much, and Kofi went to fetch a taxi.

I'd wondered if Joe even spoke English, but now it seemed he did. 'What do you do,' he said. 'What is your work?' This was a boner.

What does a secret service agent say in such circumstances? Perhaps he says he is a journalist. Joe rescued me. 'Kofi says you are a secret policeman.' I smiled weakly, non-committally. 'Please you help me, I work for oil company. Just for tonight please you say you are big American oil man, my boss. Secret police no good.' 'But why?' I said. 'Better for me,' Joe replied. 'My father, relatives very pleased big American boss come to see my mother.' I adjusted my smelly pants, and looked at my stained shirt. 'Not American,' I said, 'I'm English.' 'All right, big English oil man.' I agreed, and Kofi arrived with a very small taxi painted in black and yellow stripes like a hornet.

During the ride Joe was silent, sunk again in his sadness. I resolved to play my part manfully. I tried to pick some bits of volcanic lava off my pants, but it hadn't set properly. I wiped my glasses on Kofi's toga, and pulled up my socks. That was all I could do. We bumped along through utterly dark and deserted lanes, I'd no idea where we were, then suddenly there was a blaze of light and a burst of wild drumming: the wake for Joe's mother taking up the whole of a small alley, full of hundreds of people pressed together half-naked in the hot night. Somewhere in the middle some drummers were beating up a rhythm that got wilder. I was excited and happy as we prised our way through the crowd. A space had been cleared about half-way through the alley, and here the strangest dancing was going on. Two women, not young, with wild fuzzy hair, longer than you usually see with Africans, were stamping and leaping in what looked like a dervish dance; and that's what it was. These are devil-dancers, Kofi told me, they dance to drive the bad spirits away. The women were naked to the waist, and their breasts flopped about like pancakes. They wore grass skirts, and their black bodies were smeared with dusty white powder. They danced in short bursts of great intensity, giving sharp little barking cries, and then fell back exhausted; and then danced again. They looked very cross all the time, perhaps because of the bad spirits. Some of the crowd watched intently, stirred by the drums and the dancing; and some, as always in Africa, sat there listlessly, reading newspapers, talking, just staring around, the women feeding babies, the children playing small mysterious games with stones and squares drawn in the dirt, not knowing why they were there.

There was a hard core of mourners outside one of the houses.

Some were even weeping, and it was here that Joe and Kofi led me, and instructed me what to do. I was told to travel along the line of mourners outside the house, then into the house, up the stairs, and into the bedroom where Joe's mother lay and intimate family mourners were. With each person I must shake hands, and say a little phrase in the local dialect. Joe would go ahead to explain who I was, the great oil man, his boss. I did what I was told, shaking hands along the line of mourners, and up the stairs in the poor, ugly little house. Many were weeping, and the older ones grieved especially, those presumably who had known the old mother well. Again, I felt I was where I shouldn't be. Then Joe led me into the big upstairs bedroom where his mother was. This was the kind of epicentre of the mourning. Women and men were weeping and moaning. In the centre of the room, in a huge double bed with a crude gilt bedhead, lay the dead old lady. She seemed very dead, as if she had been dead for a long time, much longer than a day, yet she was still human all right, with a strong handsome high-boned face. Her eyes were closed and her mouth was open, filled with a sort of gag that glittered as if it was made of silver paper. She was dressed in her best, or better than her best, in a kind of bridal gown, white and silver, a beautiful dress that covered her entirely, except for that handsome head on the pillow and her gaunt hands folded in her lap. I went round the room as I had been told, shaking hands or rather holding them, murmuring the meaningless phrase of condolence that I'd been taught. Now I didn't feel an intruder any more. It seemed that I was even welcome, and not merely because I was Joe's oil man boss.

At the other end of the room there were more stairs, and we went down them and out into the alley, where the drums were drumming and the strange old women were leaping about with their breasts flapping. I felt it was time to leave, but it seemed that Joe and Kofi were coming too. I wanted a drink rather badly, but didn't like to suggest it. But I needn't have worried because Kofi did so instead. Round a couple of corners there was a European-style bar, pretty squalid actually, with tin tables and broken cane chairs, and the drinks on the shelves were European drinks, whisky, gin and beer. What would I have? I should have liked something strong, but I knew that they were poor, so I said beer. 'No, no,' said Kofi, 'you would like whisky, Scotch whisky, yes.' I said yes, all right, and three giant whiskies were poured. We sat at one of the tin tables. Joe suddenly looked less sad, and turned to me: 'Mr. Secret Police, after what you do for me tonight, I will buy for you at least one whole bottle of whisky.'

PART FOUR

HERE AND THERE

25
Five Stars Around the World
[March 1966]

IF you are ever faced with a menu in a language you don't understand a word of, try ordering a meal just on the outlandish names of the dishes. That's how I found myself a few months ago in a water-front restaurant in Reykjavik, faced with the smelliest thing I've ever had to eat: a piece of raw shark meat that had been buried in the ground for a year. The stuff is called hakarl, it's the pride of Icelandic cuisine. The smell is something like ammonia and it's so strong that when you swallow it the fumes rise from your stomach into your lungs and cause a sort of temporary suffocation from within. The effect on one's breath can be imagined, though this causes no comment in Iceland, but I got some very strange looks on the plane when I brought some of the stuff back with me. Altogether the Icelandic diet is a bit odd, with things like whale blubber (which I can compare to a rough sponge soaked in vinegar), reindeer meat (very pungent stuff) and seal's flippers (rather endearing to look at, like a baby's hands, but a bit bony to eat).

After Iceland it was bison's meat in Poland and bear's paws in Finland, but on the whole I find Europe disappointing in the out of the way eating line. America of course is rather European and Africa isn't a good eating continent. There it's either second-rate European food or dismal African dishes like the terrible 'African Chop' they're so proud of, which is nothing more than a crude curry of something like corned beef served with rice that always seems to have stones in it. Perhaps one would make an exception for the palm tree kernel salad of East Africa, made with what is literally the core of the palm tree. It's expensive, because you have to cut down the tree every time you make the salad, and I suppose you are really eating wood; but it's delicious, rather like a very pure, unfatty butter. Perhaps African food is best eaten like that, when it's not cooked. The spiced raw meat eaten in Ethiopia gets high marks from me for taste, though not for its effects on one's insides, but the staple food of the country is a sort of sour pancake called injira, which tastes exactly like damp blankets.

No, there are plenty of reasons for going to Africa, but not for food, and I wouldn't go to the Arab world for that either. I've eaten sheep's eyes with my fingers with the best of them, but eating really begins, I think, East of Suez, and in particular where the Chinese have an influence. Chinese food is absolutely the best in the world and I suppose the food capitals of the world are Hong Kong and Macao, the Portuguese colony next door. Communism struck a blow for the gourmet here. When the new régime arrived in 1949 cooks from every province of China swelled the ranks of the refugees pouring into Hong Kong, and most of them are still there. Most of the Chinese food that you get in England though, is a travesty of the real thing. You can get a better Chinese meal for a couple of shillings in a seaman's café or a street stall in Hong Kong than you can anywhere I know in London. The reason is partly that the Chinese restaurants here don't bother, they know the British will eat anything; and partly because you simply can't get a lot of the ingredients here. As you would expect from people who have starved through the centuries, the Chinese have had to have a shot at eating practically everything, things like grubs, the bark of trees, the webs of ducks' feet, rotten eggs, every kind of root and weed, and they haven't wasted their research. These things may sound disgusting, but the point is they're anything but disgusting when the Chinese have finished with them.

To whom else would it occur to make a delicious soup out of the spittle of a particular kind of bird: which is what so-called bird's-nest soup really is. They eat snakes and sea-slugs and worms and beetles, and a month or two ago in Hong Kong I was able to dine off literally legendary food: the salamander. I didn't know salamanders actually existed; they do, and there's one at the Zoo, but I didn't know that, when I discovered this one swimming around in a baby-bath on the floor of a slum restaurant, and half an hour later the poor thing lay on the table before us, in a tasty oyster sauce. The Chinese very sensibly believe in applying the butcher's knife at the last possible moment, and keep the animals alive until they're going to eat them. The idea of having dead flesh around for days, weeks and even months appals them. There is no such thing as frozen meat in China, except for what is imported for the memsahibs of Hong Kong. In Macao there is a restaurant, one of my favourites, where the tables are in the centre of the room and round the walls are ranks of cages, where the animals and reptiles gaze out, while the customers gaze in, considering these creatures from the point of view of dinner. You walk in and find an old man in a scholar's gown weighing up the merits of a cage full of lizards, while next to him some twittering Chinese ladies in cheongsams are arguing about which sauce to order with a toothsome-looking bunch of banded snakes. There are baskets with chickens and ducks trussed up inside and feeling the pinch, but any sentimental feeling for these animals is considered strictly beside the point. They are here for one purpose only: to be eaten, and the Chinese gourmet is concerned to get good value. I find I can keep up this attitude of mind just so far. Faced with a furry ant-eater curled up and waiting for the end, or a quizzical turtle paddling in his tank and giving me an eye, I am unable to pronounce sentence, and the delicacy goes to somebody else.

Perhaps this seems an almost over-exotic sort of place, but in fact the Chinese matter-of-factness about eating extends to the surroundings they eat in. What these surroundings are they don't care. If a house, as somebody said, is a machine for living in, a Chinese restaurant is a machine for eating in, utility is the yardstick, and the Hong Kong equivalent of the Tour d'Argent is a bare room with a dirty floor and glass-topped tables and pin-up girls on the walls. The kitchen is sheer squalor and chaos, and the lavatory always leads out of the kitchen. At a Chinese feast the actual eating is a messy business, and it's considered perfectly all right to chuck the bones and bits on the table-cloth. Occasionally I find myself absent-mindedly doing this in England, and it doesn't go down at all well. Chinese meals are always very jolly, even though, in Hong Kong at least, they are as often as not meals with a purpose, paid for by the expense account. Chopsticks are convivial things, and it's a beautiful sight to see a Chinese millionaire popping goodies into the mouth of another Chinese millionaire, at the same moment calculating how he can contrive to cheat and ruin him.

Chinese cuisine, though, is a cuisine without snobbery. All Chinese attach great importance to food, and even a poor man will try and eat well, though he may never get enough. If his dinner is a bowl of rice with a little fish sauce on the top, and that is dinner for plenty of people in Hong Kong, then he will make sure that the rice is good rice and the sauce fresh and the best he can get. Rice is the basis of Chinese eating. In the alleys of Hong Kong you see Chinese children squatting on their little hunkers, eating their rice with strange small chopsticks that are tipped with metal just to make them more slippery. I can't eat successfully with these at all, but Chinese children are given these specially difficult chopsticks when they are small to impress on them that it's a crime to spill even a grain of rice. It's the Chinese version of sin. If they do, mama will deliver a sharp rap over the knuckles, the only time you ever see a Chinese child being struck.

It's ironical that the most exciting and adventurous cuisine in the world should be built in this way on a sort of racial memory of poverty and starvation.

26
Letter from Iceland
[August 1965]

PEOPLE are much the same everywhere in the world, and one place is as bad as another. At least that's the way it sometimes seems to me after twenty years of travelling around. I don't really expect any longer to find the Good Society, where men live as they ought to live, but in Iceland this summer for a couple of weeks I almost had the illusion that I had stumbled on it.

There were several reasons for this, and perhaps the main one was a feeling of egalitarian living such as I hadn't had for a long time. I remember when I was first in a Communist country, in East Germany in the late forties, feeling this feeling, a strangely heady and exciting one, that for all the shabbiness and the no doubt numerous hidden injustices, this was at least a society where people were equal if only in the sense that nobody had anything. This was naïve of course, as I was very quickly made to see, and I don't think I ever had this feeling again until I went to Iceland this summer. It hasn't faded yet, though I suppose it will. I think I saw Iceland at a fortunate moment, perhaps at the last moment when this feeling of equality was possible.

W. H. Auden wrote a book about Iceland many years ago with Louis MacNeice with the same title as I've used here—'Letter from Iceland'. It's a book that conveys a lot of affection for the country, where Auden has the idea his ancestors came from, and this summer, a few weeks before I was there, Auden was back for a second visit.

He stayed a few days and when he left wrote a poem in one of the Reykjavik papers. The last lines went:

> 'O fortunate island, where all men are equal,
> But not vulgar, not yet.'

What does this nice feeling of equality stem from? The visitor's first experience of it is when he uses the telephone book. You can't ring up anybody in Iceland unless you know his Christian name since everybody is listed in the telephone book under their Christian names. This is because a man takes his father's first name as his surname, so if your father's name was, say, David Stefansson, your name would be Johannes—or some other name—Davidsson. The only way to prevent the entire population eventually having the same name has been to invent new Christian names, though this is quickly frustrated as they in turn become surnames in the very next generation. Of course we're dealing with a very small community. The whole population of Iceland is only about 180,000 and about half of these live in the capital, Reykjavik. I suppose it's a fact that you couldn't have a Good Society if you had more than a certain number of people. Perhaps a couple of hundred thousand is the biggest the family could be, and a family is just what Iceland is. Icelanders are very well behaved towards each other, and also very tolerant, and this is for the same reason that members of a family usually are. The whole country would just blow up if people weren't considerate of each other's foibles, and this makes for a very civilized atmosphere. People are pretty unshockable in Iceland and the most hair-raising behaviour is discussed with cool detachment.

I find that attitudes towards sexual behaviour are a pretty good indication of how civilized people are. In Iceland it is not so much that anything goes, as that people realize it's no good getting too steamed up about sex. The Icelanders have always been pretty promiscuous, I gather, and today the illegitimacy rate is very high indeed. This fact is a bit misleading because a lot of the children are legitimized later when their parents are old enough and working and can get married. The procedure is often for the girl's parents to take over the child, and bring him up, while she goes on with school and so on. It's the sort of thing they do in Jamaica or West Africa and seems to work perfectly well. Sometimes the couple do get married right away, and there's rather a lot of divorce in the late twenties, when the children are beginning to grow up, and the parents feel they can break up the home without too much damage to them. But then of course the children start having babies. There are plenty of thirty-year-old grandmothers in Iceland. I don't want to make jokes about this sort of thing, but the fact is that in Iceland there's absolutely no stigma attached to illegitimacy, and the cruel prejudice about bastards in our own so-called progressive society is entirely absent.

Children in Iceland grow up quickly. They seem to do some kind of job, if only in the evenings or school holidays, from a very early age, perhaps twelve or so, and Icelandic children are very independent. Crossing the country by aeroplane and bus, as I did several times, I constantly came on children making positive Odysseys by themselves, whereas in London the Kensington Mama screws up her courage to put little Johnny on a Number 11 bus. Children in Iceland actually dress like miniature adults, and I had a long conversation about politics in an aeroplane with an eleven-year-old little man wearing a Tyrolean hat with a feather in it and carrying a small briefcase.

That people in Iceland are very sure of their rights you can see by the fact that they don't insist on them, indeed never talk about them as rights. Here is a country where democracy really works. People really do consider that parliament is there to speak for them, and at elections the poll is always well over ninety per cent. There are four main parties, including a Communist Party that manages to be revolutionary and entirely respectable at the same time. Individuals have a genuine say in things. Every government minister is obliged to set aside one morning every week when anyone may go and see him with complaints or suggestions. Again Iceland has a most lively press and radio, and absolutely every issue is discussed with no holds barred. I suppose all these things sound pretty unspectacular, these are just the routine qualities of a working democracy, but one has to remember how seldom these qualities are found in action. In Iceland they do work, and the result is a kind of taste in the air, an almost palpable feeling that here are people living as we were all meant to live. I don't want to overdo this lauding of the Icelanders, and I'll go back to the point I made that this summer was probably the last moment when I could have seen this happy unspoiled state of affairs. Remember what Auden said: 'O fortunate island, where all men are equal, But not vulgar, not yet.' Not yet. But it's coming.

As well as this heady egalitarianism, the Icelanders have a very strong quality, a complimentary quality, I should say, of integrity. An Icelander knows who he is. I suppose the chief reason for this is their isolation. The first Icelanders were the Vikings, Norwegians who rebelled against the ruling chieftains in Norway, and set out across the utterly inhospitable and icy North Atlantic to find what landfall they could. When you think of their primitive long boats, their courage was staggering. Later they came again under the control of Norway and afterwards of Denmark when the centre of power in Scandinavia moved there, but Iceland was a long way from anywhere until the aeroplane, and Copenhagen's control was fairly lax. The consequence of being left alone was a quite extraordinary cultural isolation, which had some disadvantages perhaps but also terrific advantages. One is that Icelanders today speak almost exactly the same language as they spoke in the early Middle Ages, seven or eight hundred years ago. The language of the Sagas is the language of the present-day farmer and shopkeeper, of children at play or a boy and girl courting. One of the Reykjavik papers prints a daily cartoon strip featuring the heroes of the Sagas, and the balloons that come out of the characters' mouths contain not the inanities of Blondie or Perry Mason but the words of Burnt Njal or of Guthmund the Powerful. It is as though English children read Beowulf or at any rate the Canterbury Tales instead of The Beano. And on the Icelandic radio the Sagas are performed as a kind of perpetual serial, instead of Mrs. Dale or Coronation Street. It is easy to sentimentalize this kind of thing, to talk as if you only had to scratch any Icelander and you'd find a poet or a Viking, but the Sagas are wonderful literature and going so deep into Icelandic life they help to keep alive that sort of integrity I mentioned.

Of course all this integrity has its debit side, in an occasionally exaggerated conservatism. The national heritage is a long way from being fossilized, but that is always the danger: you know, compulsory reading of the Sagas and that sort of thing. Already there is legislation to prevent any Icelander giving his children a non-Icelandic name, and a solemn committee sits to invent new words for the language when they are unavoidable. The Japanese for 'jet' is 'jet', but the Icelandic is something unpronounceable by me that has no non-Icelandic origins whatever. I'm not saying this conservatism is altogether a bad thing, and up to now there's been a sense of proportion. The Icelanders see foreign influence, though, as a definite danger. It all began during the war, when Iceland was a kind of aircraft carrier for the Allies. The immediate consequences of this were good, because money came into what had been a pathetically poor country, and the end of the war gave the Icelanders the opportunity to kick out their Danish masters. They even went so far as to join NATO, though they have neither Army, Navy or Air Force. Their contribution is a barren strip of land which they have handed over to the Americans to use as a base. It is the most godawful place (called Keflavik) but 3,000 American servicemen and their families live there. The Icelanders keep them shut in, except on one day a week, when the bars in Reykjavik are closed to make sure they don't misbehave, but the Americans have a secret weapon: television. Iceland has no television, nor would you expect it in a country with a population not much larger than Brighton and Hove, but there are thousands of television sets tuned to the TV that the Americans have rigged up at Keflavik to prevent their people going mad with boredom during the dark Arctic winter. This bootleg television viewing has become a matter of national anxiety. The government and the leaders of intellectual life see their national integrity being undermined by the Bell Telephone Hour and Northern Lights Playhouse. While I was in Reykjavik there was a tremendous petition got up by all the writers and professors (they have quite a pull in Iceland) and a sort of Aldermaston march was arranged from the American base into Reykjavik in which some thousands of people took part.

To some extent it is a matter for concern. Even now more books are published in Iceland per head of the population than anywhere in the world. There has been complete literacy for more than a century, and a poet or novelist in Iceland is a man of considerable substance, not as in England a mere ornament of the gossip columns. A new book of poems by Iceland's leading poet can sell up to 20,000 copies, which is sales on a James Bond level for a population of that size. Now of course there are other things in the world besides reading, but this is a healthy state of affairs that is already being undermined. More important, the Icelanders are beginning to worry about the moral standards of their young. Once or twice a year now, almost instinctively it seems, like lemmings, thousands of Reykjavik teenagers descend simultaneously on some village or farm in the country and proceed on a two or three day orgy. Terrific boozing goes on, with the potent national spirit, brennevin, lots of sex, and a good deal of pulling down hay-ricks, slaughtering of sheep, beating up of farmers and so on. Behaviour like this was unknown in the past. I discussed this phenomenon with a number of Icelanders. On the whole a most sane attitude prevailed, the sort of attitude I'm sure we should have towards our own Mods and Rockers. Tolerance won the day. A way would be found, they said. Probably the matter would settle itself. There was no talk of prisons or reform schools. And anyway, nobody goes to prison in Iceland. Not that there isn't plenty of room at the moment. A year or so ago, in celebration of some State Visit, all the prisoners in Iceland's only prison were let out, all dozen or so of them; and they haven't managed to find anyone yet to put in their place. I believe there are a couple of murderers that they couldn't pardon, but they have their own keys, and are allowed to go home at week-ends.

27
Hearts and Minds
[April 1965]

IN the jungle clearing suddenly a great wind sprang up, blowing the trees into disarray and flattening the undergrowth. Another helicopter of 845 Squadron spiralled down on to its landing pad, marked out in the clearing with white stones like a grave. I undid the straps that held me in and climbed down from my high seat next to the pilot. Around us on the small ledge of land above the brown rushing river stood half a dozen Wessex helicopters, each in its circle of white stones. This was Nanga Ga'at, the forward base of 845 Squadron, Royal Navy, twenty miles from the border between Sarawak in Malaysia and Kalimantan or Indonesian Borneo. It didn't look like any sort of a base, except for the helicopters. A muddy path straggled away towards some grass-and-bamboo huts and that was all. My pilot swung himself down from the cockpit. 'Let's get along to the mess.' We passed between a couple of huts and bumped into a small boy with no clothes on marshalling some disgruntled pigs in front of a little wooden shack.

'Oh, that's the Chinese shop,' the pilot said, 'and that's the saw-mill down there'. He pointed to a rickety building of bamboo poles and matting. I followed him along some slippery planks laid over the mud. On one side there was a sort of enclosure made of bushes and sticks. 'That's the zoo,' he said, and inside were some chickens scrabbling and one large grey moose-like animal with a kindly face—a Sarawak mountain deer, as my guide explained. Now we could see a bit more: a hundred yards away a cluster of huts with some Borneo women cooking in big pots, and nearer, a muddy badminton court in front of a big bamboo hut on stilts, reached by an alarming bamboo bridge. This was the Mess.

Inside were a couple of pilots and mechanics dressed in the standard all-rank kit of shorts and tennis shoes and nothing else. There was a bar and a dart board and a fridge worked by kerosene, and the ceiling was adorned by a spread of bright pink parachute silk, tied to the walls all around and gathered to an apex at the centre, like a bedroom canopy in old Versailles. 'Well, how do you like it,' said one of the sailors, 'Jack's bloody boudoir!'

We had a beer and then a just about naked man came in with long blue-black hair, and ear lobes down to his shoulders and tattooed all over. He went up to one of the officers and they chattered away in what I supposed must be the Iban language, the Ibans being the local tribe in this part of the world. 'There's a party at their longhouse tonight,' the young officer said, 'some sort of festival. Would you like to go?' Well, of course I would. I was a little surprised though by all this cosy mixing with the locals because the war in Borneo has some special problems of security. To start with, it's not a war at all, or rather a war only on one side. The Indonesians, who took over the larger part of Borneo from the Dutch, seem to be at war all right with Malaysia, though they use the blanket word 'confrontation'; Malaysia on the other hand hasn't declared war on Indonesia. What this means in practice is that Indonesian guerilla parties can cross the thousand-mile border running from one end of this huge island to the other any time they like; they can shoot up a village or one of the longhouses or smuggle in saboteurs or fifth-columnists and then nip back across the border before the Malaysian forces and the Commonwealth forces helping them can do anything about it.

So the only real defence is information, you need to know when they are coming, and that's why I was surprised at first at the hobnobbing that went on with the Iban tribesmen at Nanga Ga'at. After all, information can travel in both directions, and we seemed to be laying ourselves open.

The border, like so many borders that cause trouble today, was an artificial line drawn up by the Dutch and the British in the old colonial days when we were masters of Sarawak. To the tribesmen of the mountains this line the white men drew means nothing at all.

They always lived on both sides of the line and have continued to do so today, half the Ibans in Indonesia, the other half in Malaysia, half the Dyaks or the Kelabits or Punans in one country, half in the other. For them the only country that matters is their own, the mountains of central Borneo, wherever the border may run, and certainly nobody else could be at home there.

In a lifetime of travelling, I've never seen anything so forbidding. The mountains are densely covered with primary jungle, with two and three hundred foot trees close together and fierce undergrowth twining between them. There are no roads, only narrow tracks, and most people travel by river in frail wooden longboats down roaring mountain streams with plenty of white water, and lower down treacherous sandbanks. To move about this country at all without the help of the local inhabitants is practically impossible, and by their knowledge of jungle signs they always know who is travelling about. Plainly no campaign could be successful in their territory without them on your side, and that's where the hob-nobbing at Nanga Ga'at comes in. In fact, Nanga Ga'at is the home of the Temongong Jugah or Paramount Chief of the Ibans and that's one of the reasons why it was chosen as a forward base. I had been thinking in terms of the Ibans succumbing to bribes or threats and giving away our activities to the Indonesians, who are after all no more than a stiff day's march away, but the reverse is true. This is a war where information counts for more than guns, and if you're living next door to the Paramount Chief, and sharing what you have with him and his people, it's likely that *all* his people can be won to your side, and that means a lot who live in Indonesia, who see the Indonesian soldiers every day, and who will send a runner fleet through the jungle when an attack is on the way.

What's important is that you should *really* be sharing what you have with the Chief and his people, that you should somehow be an integral part of the country you are defending, and not merely a more or less friendly occupying power. This is a keystone of Commonwealth policy in Borneo, it's something our soldiers and airmen are supposed to take as seriously as their military duties, and it's to this end that what's called the Hearts and Minds campaign was in-invented. The hearts and minds are those of the various tribespeople, and winning them is the object of the exercise. Every British soldier on arrival in Borneo is given a little green booklet written

Hearts and Minds

with the help of the redoubtable Tom Harrison, the anthropologist and inventor of Mass-Observation, who has lived in Borneo since the war and travelled all over the mountains.

It's an interesting little document that goes far beyond the usual army cautions about leaving the women alone and not trading on the black market. The booklet starts with some general advice, and I quote: 'The winning of Hearts and Minds of the peoples of Borneo is of great importance. You must treat these people as friends and with goodwill.' And a bit further on, 'A smile and a firm and friendly greeting to those whom you meet will serve to break the ice.' And when the ice has been broken there is a formidable list of Do's and Don't's. The Don't's are fairly obvious, things like 'Don't shout at people: they hate it' and 'Don't bathe or wash in the nude' (the Borneo people do but apparently they don't like to see us doing it). However, the Do's are the main thing. There's a long list of them, and they are all strictly practical. 'Do learn to speak the local language,' 'Do give help in making foot paths and bridges,' 'Do give help in killing vermin,' 'Do deliver letters to and from remote areas,' 'Do demonstrate equipment and weapons to civilians,' (this to give them the feeling that it is *their* struggle and they are trusted).

Now all this is good advice and for the best of reasons, but the question is does it work? The British soldier these days is a professional with a low view of high-falutin' or do-gooding ideas, and it's possible he might be a bit bloody-minded about all this delivering letters and killing vermin. Well, the slightly surprising answer is that the Hearts and Minds campaign is a runaway success, and looking after the locals is the favourite hobby of half the troops in Borneo. With the helicopter squadron at Nanga Ga'at it wasn't just a question of living naturally with the Ibans, as I was soon to see.

After those beers in the boudoir when I met the mountainy man with his tattoos and long hair, I was taken on a tour of the whole establishment: the operations room with maps, with place names in brightly coloured chalks (in this part of Borneo you make up your own names, because it is mostly unmapped country); in another hut the sleeping quarters, with pictures of Mum and girls from *Playboy* stuck on the wall; and in another, the dispensary, and here the medical orderly was working long after his usual hours while a queue of Iban men, women and especially children waited to be dosed with

Navy drugs. The orderly pointed out to me proudly the stack of tins of baby's milk he had managed to wheedle out of Navy stores; then we wandered on past a workshop where a Navy helicopter mechanic was repairing the rudder from a river-boat while the Iban owner helped; and on again to the little village where the Paramount Chief's retinue lived, and the children played around in the dirt, dressed almost without exception in the brightly coloured silk of parachutes once used for dropping supplies in the jungle.

There is no dusk in the tropics; suddenly it's as if a light had been switched out, and we groped our way along the mud paths back for a beer in Jack's boudoir, where the party for the longhouse was gathering. Only a few people could come, of course, because, what you forgot as you strolled round this normal Borneo village, was that this was a war, with an enemy somewhere in the jungle and perhaps at this moment watching the light of the paraffin lamp swinging above the bar, that there were six helicopters and their crews at the ready, and sentries posted all round the perimeter of the village that was also a camp.

Almost everybody goes to the longhouse, but only a few at a time, and a couple of ratings and a young Lieutenant called Neil were the only ones going with me tonight in the small boat with the outboard motor down the dark river a dozen miles to Long Jarwe. Here one hundred and fifty people live together as a family, a sort of tribe within the tribe, an entire village living in one huge long house, perched on stilts. There's an open balcony running the length of the building, behind that a long closed balcony, and behind that a dozen or so large separate rooms, where each separate family lives.

The way a party is given is for everybody to have a drink in everybody else's room, and you drink toasts with just about the whole of the longhouse in the course of the night. We were to sleep there too which seemed just as well.

We started in the headman's room, where we changed into sarongs, and I sat cross-legged while a beautiful girl in a topless dress sang a song of welcome to me, and then poured a glass of sourish rice wine down my throat. The young Lieutenant called Neil knew his Iban and he translated. It seems in the song that I was a brave helicopter pilot fighting the wicked Indonesians out of my love for the Iban people, words of flattery of course, yet in the girl's manner, in the manner of all the people in that room, there was no obsequiousness whatever.

My annoyance at not knowing the language was the worse at feeling myself in such good company; and I couldn't depend on my translator all the time. He was at a party, but he was still on duty, or rather his duty was his pleasure. When I had been adequately welcomed, the headman's family began to thin out, going to other rooms, and the elders of the longhouse came in and squatted on the floor next to the headman and the young helicopter pilot in his sarong. This was a conference, a parley, and some of it was translated for me: some progress had been made with a path through the forest to the next longhouse, thanks were given for the Squadron's assistance; then, this week a hundred and fifty rats had been killed, and the strange powder the Navy had brought had worked like magic. Then they came to the real business of the evening.

For this no translator was necessary. Paper and pencil were produced, and a moderately good drawing of an Elsan and how it works was done by young Neil, and a sort of missionary note seemed to come into his voice. The elders listened, looked questioning—what was the use of such a thing?—asked more questions, nodded, perhaps were gradually convinced; but I excused myself after a while to make a tour of the longhouse. There were more rooms, more songs from topless dresses and drinks, naked babies squalling, puppies snapping and old ladies with flapping breasts bent over stoves, and offers of more wine and little cakes twisted into strange shapes that tasted of paraffin, and in every room, inexplicably, grandfather clocks, never actually working—what Victorian super-salesman had managed to unload these?—and in every room laughing and friendly people: I was in very good company, but I didn't understand much until I found someone from the Squadron in one of the last rooms.

In his sarong he was bending over a man lying still on a grass mat, with his face in a set expression that might mean either indifference or great pain. There was a tin box open with a hypodermic and various medicines. People, I suppose the man's family, stood anxiously about. What was wrong? His boat had overturned in rapids, he was flung on the rocks, had barely been able to crawl ashore. You never think things like this, that would certainly happen to oneself in a country like Borneo, ever happen to the people who live there, but of course they do. The young Iban had broken some ribs, it seemed, and perhaps hurt himself inside too, it was hard to tell as they never complained. Would I call Neil, the young helicopter pilot? He came, and there was a conference, and a quick decision. At first light we would take the man back to Nanga Ga'at, somehow we would get him down the bank and into the boat, where he would be loaded into a helicopter and flown down to hospital at the coast, a journey that would take an hour, but an impossible fortnight of agony in an Iban river-boat. Remember the list of Do's and Don't's in the little green booklet: 'Do evacuate critically ill civilians by air and arrange for their return when cured.'

Neil announced his decision in Iban, and no one smiled or looked surprised or even relieved. Today this is what they expect; they knew that the best would be done for the sick man. Apparently the advice in the little green booklet works, and Hearts and Minds have been won in Borneo.

28
To Fly from Christmas
[December 1965]

WHY on earth did I chose to spend my first Christmas away from my parents in 1947 wandering in the Western Desert among the relics of war? From Cairo, where I had a job, I went to Alamein and beyond, five years after the battle I was too young to be in, and spent Christmas day driving through the tawny Egyptian desert still cluttered with the rubbish of war, climbing over sandbags and abandoned guns and into smashed tanks with things still inside that I shrank from. Why did I want to spend Christmas day like that? Why the following year was I on a Greek island, alone in a cold home in a howling gale, and all the more alone for not speaking more than a few words of Greek; and the following year, back in Egypt, exploring the strange salt marshes of Mariut outside Alexandria by myself, the lonely place described in Lawrence Durrell's *Justine*? The point was not so much, I think, to be far away, because I always like that, and spend half my life trying to be. Perhaps the idea was to be alone, away from the crass jollity of Christmas, but I'm not sure about that either. Christmas needn't always be crass and usually I'm asked by nice friends to their nice parties. A few years ago I was staying with just such people in a house high over Dublin Bay, yet I let them go off to an absolutely splendid party on Christmas day, and spent the afternoon by myself, not at all lonely, in the pleasant house high on Howth Head, reading and playing records, watching the waves wrinkling in the bay below, and the clouds high over Wicklow.

Four years ago my Christmas was even more weirdly isolated. I found myself in London on Christmas morning, God knows why but I think I had been broadcasting the previous evening, but I pretty soon saw I had to get out of the place. I rang round the airlines, but there was nobody there. Finally I found an office that was open, and a sulky Christmas voice on the phone, and in fact there was a flight, only one flight the whole day, and that was to Amsterdam. Well, I like Amsterdam, so I made a booking. At London Airport there was no traffic pile-up in front of the terminal, and the vast terminal itself was quite empty. Another sulky man looked at my passport, and a cross girl told me where to wait. Beyond the terminal, dozens, scores of aircraft stood around on the tarmac. I've never seen anything like so many before. Nobody, of course, flies anywhere on Christmas Day. There were no mechanics milling around, no passenger buses weaving among the planes, none of those contraptions that do the refuelling, no activity at all. The whole scene was like how the world is apparently meant to look after the cobalt bomb is dropped, that wicked development of the H-bomb that is going to annihilate all the people but leave the things intact for the conqueror to use. I felt like the forward scout of an invading army; or like the only man in the world. I couldn't have felt less Christmassy.

When the cross girl called me to my flight, suddenly three very small Japanese appeared from nowhere, carrying briefcases and cameras, wearing dark glasses on this dull winter day, looking like figures in a puppet play. We marched out to the aircraft, the four of us, three Buddhists and myself, the only people in London who didn't give a damn for Christmas. But is that true? I'm not a Christian, but even I have had my Christian Christmases. Last year, for instance, I arrived in Warsaw on Christmas morning, after driving 300 miles in a small sports car in the dark on icy roads. I was dead tired, and I wasn't sure what to expect. Poland is a Communist country, but it's a Catholic one too. What would Christmas Day in Warsaw be like? Would people be going to work as usual, perhaps dropping in to church on the way? Or would it be a holiday without any holiday feeling, the streets as dead and cold and deserted as in London? Well, the streets were deserted, because there are so few cars in Poland, but the pavements were crowded as I drove through the cold grey city, and the people were dressed as well and as gaily as they can afford to be, and they were crowding into the churches; so I left the car, without bothering about a hotel yet, and went to church myself, shaggy and unshaven as I was, in the great cathedral in Novy Swiat Street. The cathedral was packed. At the back the people were so close together they could not kneel. Perhaps half of them were young, under twenty-one, and they were all concentrated on one thing only, the altar. The splendour of the cathedral was a great contrast to the shabbiness of the congregation, even dressed in their Christmas best as they were. Here I felt was religion in action in a way we have forgotten in this country, and I was moved, and glad to be moved. It was something like what I'd felt nearly ten years before in Peking where I'd gone to escape the proprieties of a colonial Christmas in Hong Kong. Religion of course is not allowed on the whole in Communist China, but the old Catholic Cathedral in Peking is let function, for the sake of foreigners, and to keep up a pretence of tolerance. The Chinese Christians that are left don't dare to go very often, but on Christmas Day 1957, that church was crowded, and the people who came to worship took no notice of the men who were pointed out to me at the door, the men from the Party who stood and watched who went in. I was moved again, as who wouldn't be; but religion, even for the irreligious like myself, isn't just a matter of watching other people being religious.

I remember a Christmas in the Aran Islands off the West of Ireland, actually on the island of Inisheer, the small one where people are most like they used to be. Inisheer today is beginning to be corrupted by the Admass world that has swallowed us all up, but in 1952 the place was almost as it had been in the days when J. M. Synge wrote *The Playboy of the Western World* about these same Aran people. I arrived at Inisheer on Christmas Eve on the old steamer from Galway, and was rowed ashore by the fishermen in a canvas-bottomed curragh through the alarming Atlantic waves. There was no hotel, so I found a room in the house of a fisherman's widow, Mrs. Connely I think, who took in the rare visitors. The next day I got up early to watch the church-going. Every single person on the island filed through the little haphazard village to the one church. They weren't dressed in anything special. They went into the church, and I would have liked to follow them, but I felt out of place, I had no place there. I stood in the wind near the church, watching the sea, and wondered why the church was so silent and the service hadn't apparently begun. Then round the headland of the beach appeared a curragh, rowed by four strong islanders with a priest in his habit sitting in the bows. There was only one priest, I remembered then, for the two adjacent islands of Inishmaan and Inisheer, and so he had to celebrate two Christmasses that day.

When the service began, I walked away down the beach and over the dunes towards the rocks where the Atlantic crashes down on this bare island. I saw a graveyard, and I like graveyards, so I went to explore the tombstones for half an hour, reading there of death at sea over and over again, and the ages much too young, and then I noticed a hollow in the graveyard and went to investigate. The hollow was a very old church, or chapel, that had been buried in the sand of the dunes, except that the people had scooped the sand out of the building, which was bare and empty. I jumped down into the tiny square. It was only a few steps to walk round the whole place. It was quite empty, and I could see where the altar had been, and by scraping away some caked sand, I gradually uncovered a Christ figure cut in the stone above the altar and worn away now almost to nothing. What a strange Christ this was! More like a monkey than a man. He'd been put there perhaps two hundred years before by some fisherman-artist whose only talent had been his faith, but the faith of people in places like Aran is fuelled by a life more intense and closer to what I'd call the facts of life than our own, and this unknown artist had managed to express in that monkey figure the two things he knew about Christ, namely, that he loved and suffered. Perhaps it was more an Easter figure than a Christmas one, but it made that Christmas for me.

I'm afraid my Christmasses sound a bit lugubrious, with me always wandering about outside by myself and out of things, whereas I'd be perfectly welcome to come in and join the feast. It's old Scrooge again; but not really. Even the solitary thing isn't a simple avoidance of other people. I've had some fine Christmas parties. Three years ago I was in East Africa and on Christmas morning I found myself arriving by lake steamer at Mwanza on Lake Victoria. Tanganyika is my home and the place I like better than anywhere, and I stepped ashore in the usual proprietary way I feel when I return to that country. I found my way to the train, and we were off on the 60 hours' journey to Dar-es-Salaam. It's only about 900 miles, but I had thought of this long, slow saunter through the great central plain of Tanganyika as being (among other things) a good way to dodge Boxing Day as well as Christmas, and so miss the whole Christmas thing.

It turned out much more fun than that. I was travelling First Class, because I am getting a bit old to sleep on the floor among the chickens and babies in an African railway carriage, but I was a bit worried that this would deprive me of African company, and I certainly didn't want to spend two and a half days in the company of a Scottish missionary or an English commercial traveller; but I needn't have worried. Perhaps because it was Christmas and a few travellers, the rest of the First Class had been commandeered by the train crew, and we hadn't gone far out of Mwanza before I was playing poker with the relief engine driver and a couple of the dining room stewards. This arrangement turned out to have quite a few advantages, such as that beer was available at any hour of the day or night, and also that the train could be stopped at will. I had no particular reason to stop in the middle of the bundu, but after a couple of days during which he won about two pounds ten off me, the relief driver, my great friend by this time, felt apparently he should do me a service in return.

Just after Movogoro, at about one in the morning, I woke to find the train stationary and this driver chap at my elbow in the dark. He was asking me to get up, almost telling me. I tried not to listen to him, but he went on talking. I cursed him, but still he continued. I had to listen. We had stopped, he said, at his own village. This was not allowed, but nobody would know. He would like to give me some 'Christmas', he said. I wanted Christmas even less than to be woken up, and Christmas was yesterday, I said, but in Africa you have to accept this sort of situation, and I pulled on my pants and we tramped off into the night, leaving the train, an engine and a dozen carriages, just standing there with the passengers chatting unconcernedly in the dark.

A couple of hundred yards and we came to a huddle of huts with a few petrol lamps burning. There were greetings and whisperings and a gabble of Swahili and people shunting me around and eventually I was led into a hut by my driver friend, and there Christmas was in the hot small smelly hut: in the shadows on the mud floor, black babies squealing; a calabash of beer spilled but another mercifully upright and full; huge ladies in ballooning print dresses laughing and thrusting clay mugs of sour beer at me; the petrol lamps swinging dangerously under the thatch; my friend the relief driver and his brothers and cousins and aunts and friends; all of us having Christmas a day late in the dark in the middle of Africa. Well that was Tanganyika three years ago; last year it was Warsaw in the cold; the year before Berlin; and now in 1965, as you hear this, I'm delighted to say I'm spending my Christmas in the gay and gaudy island of Haiti where the voodoo is.

29
Conrad on the Spot
[December 1966]

THIS is a strange story I want to tell; strange only because of a coincidence I'm sure, but strange all the same to me. It was in Bangkok about eight years ago. For a couple of years I'd travelled around the Far East and now I was making a last goodbye journey to Thailand and Malaya before going home to England. I had friends in Bangkok and I spent a couple of days with them, tasting the pleasures of that happy city for the last time. On the evening of the second day I was to take a boat down the Chao Phya river (that Bangkok is on) to the Gulf of Siam and on to Malaya. After I'd done my final rounds and bought some sort of a book to read on the boat, I had one last afternoon to spend with a friend in what we called the Garden Room. The charm of the Garden Room was that though it was bang in the middle of Bangkok, by some freak, the noises of that noisy city were muted and made to seem far away so they even had a sort of glamour, the glamour of the busy world when you don't have to be busy yourself. The Garden Room used to be an opium den. It's a balcony round two sides of a courtyard, and the shutters that used to close the balcony in were open now, and we would lie inside on the old opium couches and not smoke opium, because that wasn't allowed any more, but lean back and drink Chinese tea and talk and look down into the courtyard and listen to the birds singing in the trees there.

My friend Jan is a Dutchman who taught in those days at the University in Bangkok. He's one of those Europeans who many years ago took a slow boat to China and never came back—enchanted by the grace and sanity and sheer gift for living that Asians seem to possess. For the past few years he'd come to rest among the gentle Thais. In those days I used to read Joseph Conrad a lot, who wrote so wonderfully about that part of the world, and my friend Jan always reminded me of Conrad's novel *Victory*, of the character Heyst, the Swedish exile in the story, who had found the same rapport with the East, who like Jan was a solitary who found his need for solitude answered by Asian behaviour—that odd mixture of intimacy and reserve so unlike the neurotic clamour of Western relationships.

We lay on the hard wood of the opium couch and talked in a desultory way. Jan had brought a bottle of whisky as a present for my journey and we put a little of it in our tea as we talked: about his work and my journeys, about mutual friends, and about Conrad. I told him, not for the first time, how he reminded me of Heyst, and we talked about the Conrad world that we'd both seen something of: the rivers of North Borneo where Almayer pursued his folly; Raffles Quay in Singapore, in many ways so little changed; and the lovely fishing villages of the East coast of Malaya, not changed at all. There was one place though that I couldn't identify, and I'd been trying to for a year. I couldn't even remember the name of the Conrad story (or, rather, 'tale' as he used to call them) where the place is described.

In the Garden Room I tried to tell this story to my friend. It takes place, I told him, in the mouth of a winding river, like one of those curly Borneo rivers, and the storyteller is a sea-captain like Conrad himself. There's a ship, anchored, with the captain on deck, and they're waiting for a wind. Until then they can't set sail, so the captain dismisses his crew and takes the watch himself, pacing the deck and looking at the scene as the sun sets. There are some bamboo fish traps sticking out of the water of the kind you see all over South East Asia, and some rocky islands nearby, and the sea is dead flat under the huge sky and the land on the margins of the sea nearly as flat. Everything is still. Pacing the deck the captain reaches down to pull up a rope ladder that's carelessly been left over the side, but there's some resistance, and he finds to his surprise in this empty place that there's a naked swimmer hanging on the ladder.

As I told the tale I watched my friend for a clue. He knew his Conrad and he ought to know the story and perhaps even the place where it was set; but apparently not. We sprawled on our couch and Jan poured some more tea and I added a little whisky, and I went on. I told how the captain of the ship helped the swimmer on board, and then for some reason didn't call out the crew but took the man down to his cabin and gave him clothes and food and listened to his strange visitor's strange story. They sat in the old-fashioned panelled cabin and the stranger told the captain he was a seaman who had jumped overboard from another ship and could never go back because he had killed a man. The captain was an upright young fellow, he had the Conrad sense of honour, but he also had the Conrad sense of guilt, that doesn't allow a man to blame another man for even something like murder, for we all carry evil inside us and so easily we could be the murderer. So the captain keeps his visitor hidden in his cabin, and at the end of the tale he lets him loose, to swim free to whatever his destiny may be.

My friend Jan listened to all this, but he couldn't remember the story, let alone the place where it was set; and the time was getting on, I had my boat to catch to sail down the river and on to Malaya, so we finished the tea and I put the cork back in the whisky. We left the Garden House and he drove me down to the boat where we said goodbye.

It was an odd little steam boat, only a couple of hundred tons and at least thirty years old, and I had to step down from the quayside to get on deck, where I was met by the Danish captain who took me to my cabin, a small oak-panelled room with a chronometer let into the wall. When I came back on deck it was dark and we were moving downstream and a supper of Chinese noodles and American corned beef was laid out for me to share with the Dane. We washed the taste of that away with my whisky, and sat and talked while the native fishing boats went by on the river with their lights bobbing and voices calling, and when the moon came out we could see the palms along the shore standing like asterisks against the sky; but I wasn't good company, I didn't feel like talking, and when the bottle was empty I went to bed and hoped that the drumming of the engines would send me to sleep. I slept, and woke at first light, knowing I wouldn't sleep again. The ship was still now, and I lay in my boxed-in bunk and looked round the cabin, and thought how like the captain's cabin in that Conrad story this was, with the old-fashioned oak-panelling and the chronometer let into the wall. I'm sure he had a chronometer; that is if he existed. I'd had that story on my mind for a year, and I was beginning to think I'd made the whole thing up. A good cure for thinking gloomy thoughts in bed is to get up and get dressed.

I did that thing, and looked out of the porthole but there was nothing to see except sea, so I put a book in my pocket and went on deck to try if I could raise some tea. On the deck I looked around. We were anchored in the mouth of the Chao Phya river, at the head of the Gulf of Siam. I hadn't ever been here before, but somehow the scene wasn't strange. We were anchored a few hundred yards offshore, and everything was very still and quiet. There was nothing much to see; only a few bamboo fish-traps sticking out of the water of the sort you see all over South East Asia, and a little group of bare rocky islands nearby, and the sea was dead flat and very blue under the huge early morning sky and the land on the edge of the sea was nearly as flat. I had a great feeling of strangeness, and for a moment didn't know why. A Malay boatboy came on deck and I sent him to make some tea. I walked round the deck and looked at everything again, and then I sat on a stanchion and got out the book I'd bought in Bangkok. It was all I'd been able to find, a paperback with a crude bosomy cover and the title *Great Short Stories of the World*. I opened the book and the first story was called 'The Secret Sharer' by Joseph Conrad. I began at the beginning: 'On my right hand there were lines of fishing-stakes resembling half-submerged bamboo fences, and to the left a group of barren islets set in a blue sea that itself looked solid, so still and stable did it lie below my feet. I turned my head and saw the straight line of the flat shore joined to the stable sea, with a perfect and unmarked closeness, in one levelled floor, half brown, half blue under the enormous dome of the sky. Two small clumps of trees, one on each side of the only fault in the impeccable joint, marked the mouth of the river we had just left on the first stage of our homeward journey. Apart from that, I was alone, alone with my ship, anchored at the head of the Gulf of Siam. She floated at the starting-point of a long journey, very still in an immense stillness, the shadows of her spars flung far to the eastward by the setting sun.'

30
The Pleasure of Contrast
[March 1966]

'You're in the Errol Flynn suite, sir,' said the manager, and a little black Jamaican bell-boy took my rather shabby bag and led the way. The Errol Flynn suite was rather grand, with a gold telephone and a satin bedhead to the enormous bed and a signed picture of Errol Flynn on the wall. 'Did Errol Flynn really sleep here?' I asked the bell-boy. 'Yes, sah,' he said, looking reproachfully at the shilling I had nervously tipped him. I took off my clothes, and put on swimming trunks and went down to the bar. At the Jamaica Reef hotel there is a swimming pool *in* the bar. There were a couple of gorgeous American girls splashing around, so I splashed too and then sat on the edge and drank a Planter's Punch with a large cherry on the top. Then I changed and joined my companions for dinner out on the terrace under the stars at a table lit by a candle in a ship's lantern. The wine was vintage and we ate dolphin steaks. This is the life, I thought. The talk was all pure James Bond stuff about deep sea fishing and water skiing and underwater exploration for treasure. I looked back on the day since we'd landed at Montego Bay after drinking champagne all the way from New York in the VC-10. Montego Bay was a bit of a flop I thought, in spite of the posh hotels and the American girls in their handsome tans and the heady air of money being spent like water. The drive along the coast was superb. The North Shore of Jamaica is really one of the smashing places of the world, a sort of South Seas dream come true.

We were to have lunch at the Playboy Hotel at Ocho Rios, in the Bunny Club. I'd never seen a Bunny in the flesh, so this was a great moment. To my mind the Playboy Hotel must be one of the ugliest buildings in existence, of a surpassing ugliness that takes on a sort of grotesque beauty. We had a bathe in the pool, and stared at the Bunnies with their floppy silk ears and bow ties and fluffy tails. I was a bit disappointed that they looked like any other girls. After lunch we were shown around the whole splendid and absurd establishment. Up in the penthouse were the Bunnies' quarters, guarded by a monster Negro also straight out of James Bond. On the notice board was pinned the Bunny Code, a formidable list of rules to keep the Bunnies in order. We were introduced to the Bunny Mother, a not particularly matronly lady who would have made quite a Bunny herself. 'You've read the Bunny Code,' she said. 'These Bunnies couldn't be safer in their own homes.' I read the rules again. They were mostly Don't's. 'Don't drink during working hours; Don't fight on club property; No immoral conduct on club property; no obscene language in club area; Don't loaf on the job; Don't sleep on the job; Don't come to work while still under the effects of excessive drinking.' I thought the Code painted a rather lurid picture by implication of the off duty life of the Bunnies, but the Bunny Mother didn't agree.

We went into a room where a Bunny was showing lantern slides on the wall to a group of other Bunnies sitting on the floor. The pictures were all of Bunnies. 'This is Bunny School,' said the Bunny Mother. 'There's a right and a wrong way to do everything that a Bunny has to do. Our Bunnies are all carefully trained.' The Bunny teacher had been reading instructions apposite to the slides out of a big blue manual. I edged over and tried to read over her shoulder, but she slid the manual out of sight like the plans of a secret weapon. I noticed that the Bunnies on the floor were all black or brown Bunnies, Jamaican girls, and far prettier than the pale and rather goose-pimpled Bunnies round the swimming pool. 'Yes, we're taking in some Jamaican Bunnies now,' said the Bunny Mother. 'At first we had to be a bit careful. Jamaican girls are inclined to get fresh with the guests. I guess they don't have the reserve of American girls.' She explained that all new Bunnies are sent to Chicago for a sort of brainwashing (or I suppose you would say sex-washing) course, where they get all that nonsense knocked out of them. We left the Bunnies to their magic lantern show, and stepped out into the sunshine. Behind I could hear the Bunny teacher starting up again: 'Now, Bunnies, we come to the Bunny Bob . . .'

We drove on in the sunshine in our huge American car with the top down, and the scenery was a dream of white beaches and turquoise sea with the waves breaking steadily on the coral reef. We sailed past Discovery Bay, where Columbus landed, and Runaway Bay, where the Spaniards fled when the British moved in. Jamaica has a rich and extraordinarily romantic history, but the place names are out of another and perfectly familiar world. We drove through St. Ann's Bay and Albany and Highgate and Windsor Castle and Bonnie View until we got to Port Antonio, where I was to sleep in Errol Flynn's bed. The next day we were to visit an even grander establishment, indeed just about the grandest hotel in the world, or at any rate the most expensive. This is Frenchman's Cove, five or six miles from Port Antonio, where Garfield Weston, the Canadian millionaire, caters for his peers. It's just a little place where a millionaire can go and get away from it all in the company of his own sort of folk. Breakfast at Port Antonio was an extension of the euphoria of the evening before: papaya and avocado and eggs and bacon and Blue Mountain coffee on the terrace looking down at the surf creaming on an impossibly white beach. This is the life, I thought again.

After breakfast we drove on to Frenchman's Cove. It wasn't quite what I expected. It's less a hotel than a sort of village. If you're a paying guest, which I was not, you drive in to a gate house where you hand over your car and are given a little electric sort of wheel chair in exchange. This is your transport while you're at Frenchman's Cove. Wandering among lakes and trees and flowerbeds in forty acres of clever landscaping are little asphalt paths leading to cottages placed with a view of the sea. There's a central house where you take your meals. It's all very expensive, but there's no nonsense at Frenchman's Cove about signing chits or making up bills at the end. Nor do you need money at Frenchman's, merely a cheque-book. Everybody pays the same, roughly a thousand pounds a fortnight for a couple, or about thirty-five pounds per day per person. For this you can have anything you want: Champagne galore, any earthly thing you like to eat (there's no menu, you just order what you want), caviare by the bucket, telephone calls to anywhere in the world, a plane to fly you round the island, a cabin cruiser to go deep sea fishing. If this isn't enough, if you don't *like* Frenchman's Cove, you can even go and stay at another hotel, and Frenchman's will pay the bill.

Obviously this was the ultimate in the dream life I seemed to be living, and also quite a challenge. Caviare and champagne and phone calls to London seemed too tame, so when I was asked what wish I had that Frenchman's could grant, I thought furiously. I needed a trump card and suddenly I had one. When I was last at the Ritz in London, I'd made a great discovery, that the Ritz—as far as I know at any rate—is the only restaurant where you can get tapioca pudding, a dish that most people see the last of when they leave the nursery. Now I happen to like, even dote on, tapioca pudding, and I could think of nothing more euphoric than to tuck into a big plate of the gorgeous gummy stuff while all around me were filling themselves with caviare. If I couldn't have this, at least I would have outfaced the management of Frenchman's Cove with this outrageous request. So I asked: Tapioca, please; and 'Yes, sah', said the waiter and wanted to know how I liked it done. I looked out of the window and there was an old Spanish Main cannon standing on the lawn. 'Anything else, sah,' said the waiter at my side. 'Yes, get me Miss Jamaica,' I said in desperation, 'and we'll fire her out of the cannon.' 'Yes, sah,' he said unperturbed, but she never came.

I walked down to the beach, which must be the most perfect beach on earth. The water is Grotto Blue. The palm trees lean at all the right angles, as though they'd been put there by Cecil Beaton. The sand is swept every day and any leaves or twigs removed. On the beach was Mr. Garfield Weston, who runs Frenchman's Cove. 'What do you think of the place?' he asked. I expressed awe and wonderment. 'Actually,' he said, 'the people who come here aren't very demanding. They like simple things. They like to do things for themselves. One man cooked all his own meals. He said he never got a chance to do that at home. We like to give them every consideration. That's what's so special about Frenchman's Cove: the special attention our guests get. TLC we call it: Tender Loving Care, you know.' I was beginning to find the Tender Loving Care a bit stifling, so I got on my little electric car, and drove along the paths to my big American one, and drove to Port Antonio and on to Kingston, where the other half lives. I have a theory about travel—

rather an ordinary one—that the pleasure lies in contrast. Nobody wants to lead the high life all the time, or you become blunted and cease to realize that it *is* the high life. Nobody wants to live in squalor all the time either, but there is a certain honesty about squalor, squalor is maybe a little nearer reality, and certainly most people in the world live in squalor; and I began to feel at Frenchman's Cove that it was time for a little squalor.

There are few more squalid places than Kingston, the capital of Jamaica. The setting of hills and sea may be perfect, but downtown Kingston is an abomination to the eye and the nose. At least it would have been to the guests at Frenchman's Cove, but I have a certain taste for ramshackle streets and ramshackle people, and in small dirty unconsidered bars you can sometimes find (as I've said) that certain honesty and reality. That's why I went to Sammy's Bar in the warren of streets at the back of Harbour Street. Sammy's was no different from dozens of other rum shops: it was just the one I happened to go into. Behind the bar was a big notice: 'Please Pay As You Are Serve. Idlers Keep Out.' The bar appeared to serve nothing but rum and beer. At one end a schoolgirl was doing her homework, writing awkwardly and with vast concentration, so that her tongue was hanging out. In a corner some tough-looking chaps were playing bar billiards. 'One quart of rum to anyone knocking four pins down' said a notice above the table. I ordered a rum myself. 'White rum, sah?' said the barman, and pointed to a bottle of colourless liquid with 'Overproof' written on it large. Overproof: why not, I thought, and the fiery stuff hit me like a fist in the chest.

I sat there sipping, and suddenly sitting beside me was a most singular fellow. He was tall, and dressed in rags, and he stank. There was nothing singular about that in this part of Kingston. What was special about this man was his hair, frizzy in the Negro fashion of course, but long and dyed a sort of rust red, curling down to his shoulders in Shirley Temple ringlets and quite indescribably filthy. He nodded to me rather haughtily and drank a rum. Now I knew what he was, from his appearance: a Rastafarian, a member of a religious sect in Jamaica who do not cut their hair or wash because they believe the Bible doesn't allow it. The Rastas (as they are usually called) are a most peculiar lot of fellows, and I'd heard stories that made me curious. They've got a bad name, because they're supposed to smoke marijuana, harbour violent racial beliefs. It was on these that I tried to draw my bar companion out. It took a long time and a lot of rum. Rastas are suspicious of white people, and they have some weird ideas about them. They believe that the white world and the black are forever separated. The white world is ruled over by the Pope who is also the head of the Ku Klux Klan. The English branch is ruled by the Queen who is the reincarnation of Philip of Spain. There's no place in this set-up for black men, and they should all go back to Africa, where their great leader is Haile Selassie of Ethiopia, the Ras Tafari as they call him. Of course the Ethiopians are not Negroes at all, but this doesn't worry these chaps.

My man at the bar began to talk. It wasn't very coherent, because the rum was taking effect and I rather think from a sort of unaired odour about him that he'd been smoking marijuana. He wasn't shy in talking about that. God, he said, smoked marijuana too. God, of course, was black. White men were evil by definition, but my companion told me this with a disarming lack of personal animosity. I was fundamentally evil and anti-Christ; and he bought me a rum and shook with laughter. He said he was going to emigrate to Ethiopia, that the whole population of Jamaica would be emigrating, that they would leave this cursed island to the tourists on the North Shore. I said I thought it was a very nice island, and not only the North Shore. He said the government of Jamaica was a bunch of rascals who had usurped the authority of Haile Selassie. I said Jamaica seemed to me to be a civilized and well-run country. He said the Jamaicans were a bunch of Godless barbarians. I said they were about the most charming people I have ever met. In this ridiculous way we squabbled amiably for a couple of hours. I didn't know much more at the end about the Rastas, except to be sure they *were* a very odd lot. The schoolgirl finished her homework and went away. The bar billiards concluded without anyone winning that quart of rum, which was probably as well. Finally with some trouble I extricated myself from my madman with the Shirley Temple curls and wandered back to my hotel.

The streets were still crowded near midnight, with children screaming and bowling hoops, and families sitting on doorsteps gossiping, and broken down houses with light peeping out from a thousand cracks, and all the rum shops full and transistors blaring out calypsos. That Rastafarian was a man who inhabited a different world from the Bunny Mother, but it was nice to think at the end of my day of contrast that I didn't have to decide which was living in the real world of Jamaica, because quite certainly neither was.